The New Americans
Recent Immigration and American Society

Edited by
Carola Suárez-Orozco and Marcelo Suárez-Orozco

A Series from LFB Scholarly

The Occupational Attainment of Caribbean Immigrants in the United States, Canada, and England

Melonie P. Heron

LFB Scholarly Publishing LLC
New York 2001

Library of Congress Cataloging-in-Publication Data

Heron, Melonie P.
 The occupational attainment of Caribbean immigrants in the
United States, Canada, and England / Melonie P. Heron.
   p. cm. -- (The new Americans)
Includes bibliographical references (p.) and index.
 ISBN 1-931202-20-6 (alk. paper)
 1. Minorities--Education--Cross-cultural studies. 2.
Immigrants--Education--Cross-cultural studies. 3. West
Indians--Education--Cross-cultural studies. 4. Occupational
mobility--Cross-cultural studies. I. Title. II. New Americans
(LFB Scholarly Publishing LLC)
  LC3719 .H47 2001
  305.9--dc21

2001004866

ISBN 1-931202-20-6

Printed on acid-free 250-year-life paper.

Manufactured in the United States of America.

Table of Contents

List of Tables

Acknowledgments

I am indebted to Gordon De Jong, Mark Hayward, Leif Jensen, Nancy Landale, and Marylee Taylor for their guidance and training during my graduate tenure at The Pennsylvania State University. Special thanks to my advisors Gordon and Mark for their personal and professional support.

I am extremely grateful for the enabling love and encouragement of my family members Alma Heron, Horrice Heron, Deborah Heron-Green, Kirk Green, Grace Heron-Nolan and O. Kenneth Nolan. Their contribution to my completion of this book is immeasurable.

I am truly appreciative of Roy and Glynis Austin, Jacinta Bronte-Tinkew, Quynh-Giang Tran, Julie Kraut, and Paul Riggs, whose close friendship, support and advice have helped to sustain me. Special thanks to friends Dereck Skeete, Samantha Friedman, Deborah Graefe, Bridget Gorman, Dana Haynie, Lynette Hoelter, Debbie Blackwell, Stephanie Bohon, Trudy Suchan, and Erica Gardner for providing me with assistance, companionship, or encouragement during various stages of writing.

I would also like to thank the following faculty or staff of the Population Research Institute, University Park, PA: computer programmers Don Gensimore and Jeanne Spicer for their invaluable contributions to my research; Mike Zimmerman, Paul Riggs, Lisa and Joe Broniszewski, Stephen Matthews, and Sherry Yocum for their technical/computer, informational, and administrative support; and Suetling Pong and Glenn Firebaugh for their statistical assistance.

Thanks to: Madeline and Warren Kalbach of the University of Calgary, Canada for their useful insights into Canadian ethnic statistics; Lori Wilkinson of the University of Alberta, Canada for special ethnic tabulations; and Suzanne Model, the University of Massachusetts-Amherst for providing codes for the creation of the 1990 U.S. International Socioeconomic Index of Occupations (ISEI); and Larry Hazelrigg, Monica Boyd, John Myles and John Reynolds of the Florida State University for helpful feedback.

A subset of these analyses is based on Statistics Canada's Public Use Microdata File (PUMF) which contains anonymized individual data collected in the 1991 Census of Population. All computations on these microdata were prepared at the Pennsylvania State University and the responsibility for the use and interpretation of these data is entirely that of the author.

Some analyses were also based on the 1991 Sample of Anonymised Records (SARs) provided through the Census Microdata Unit of the University of Manchester with the support of ESRC/JISC/DENI.

Partial support for this research was provided by 1997-1998 doctoral dissertation research grants from the National Science Foundation and the Social Science Research Council.

CHAPTER 1
Introduction

I advance the scholarship on immigrant adaptation by examining the extent to which education differentially counteracts the negative effects of being black, immigrant, and female on socioeconomic achievement in the United States, Canada and England. Education is increasingly important for the upward mobility of minorities, and many scholars agree on its role as a social leveler. Immigrant status, gender, and race are three major bases of stratification documented in previous research. However, these three bases of inequality rarely operate independently. Combinations of disadvantaged statuses produce handicaps beyond those experienced by individuals with a single disadvantaged status. Interestingly, most analytic models of immigrant socioeconomic attainment have not incorporated this complex reality. I address this shortcoming by exploring interactive models of the occupational attainment of West Indian immigrants, with emphasis on the role that education plays in mitigating disadvantage.[1]

I use the migration systems framework as an orienting approach to the study of the economic adaptation of Anglophone Caribbean migrants. The migration systems approach emphasizes micro and macro links between societies sustained by large migration flows and counterflows within a network of countries. These links include historical, political, economic and societal relations which affect the size, direction and persistence of migration streams (Fawcett, 1989; Boyd, 1989; Bilsborrow and Zlotnick, 1994). On the basis of various historical and present-day linkages, as well as patterns of population movement, I establish the United States, Canada, England, and the Anglophone Caribbean as a migration system. In this

1

system, the direction and size of migrant flows from the Caribbean to a particular destination country are greatly affected by what is happening in the other destination countries. For example, the United States' Walter-McCarran Act of 1952 ended the immigration of West Indians under the quota for Britain and placed a limit of 100 on per-country immigration from the West Indies (Segal, 1987). The restrictiveness of this policy change, coupled with an open-door policy in England at the same time, was followed by high migration to England from the British Commonwealth (Foner, 1983; Segal, 1987). After British immigration policy virtually closed the door on immigration in 1962 and the U.S. and Canada liberalized their immigration policies in the mid-1960s, the Caribbean migration stream was diverted to the U.S. and Canada.

The embeddedness in a larger inter-country system of relations of Caribbean outmigration to a specific destination country sets the stage for a comparative analysis of what could be seen as the second half of the migration process--immigrant adaptation. I focus on the United States, Canada and England as the primary receiving countries of West Indians and examine the adaptation experiences of Caribbean migrants in a larger global context. How similar or different are the occupational experiences of West Indians across countries? Does education play the same role cross-nationally in influencing economic adaptation? Or does education differentially counteract the negative effects of having various combinations of disadvantaged statuses? How may differences in national economic and socio-political contexts of destination countries inform cross-national differences in immigrants' economic outcomes? For example, if receiving countries differ in their receptivity to immigrants, and to immigrants of color, in particular, can we expect that economic outcomes of black immigrants will be poorer in countries that have been less receptive or facilitating?

I analyze 1990 and 1991 census data from the U.S., Canada and England. Results show that besides having positive, additive, net effects on occupational attainment, educational qualifications are instrumental in counteracting the negative impact of disadvantaged statuses in the U.S. That is, only in the U.S. does education provide an even greater reward to occupational attainment over and above that provided on average. Interestingly, education is far more beneficial for women than for men.

This may be a function of the U.S.' transition to a service economy, which has generated more jobs for women than men and allowed native women to make significant progress in employers' job queues. In addition, education is more effective in counteracting disadvantage for African-American women than for black Caribbean women. It allows highly educated African-American, but not Caribbean, women to achieve occupational parity with highly educated white U.S.-born women. This suggests that black, English-speaking, immigrant women encounter additional barriers in the labor market relative to African-American women.

BACKGROUND

West Indian migration to the U.S., Canada and England has increased dramatically since the 1930s. Consequently, Caribbean immigrants, together with natives of Caribbean ancestry, have become a more visible minority group. Over the past few decades, they have had growing demographic, political, cultural, and economic impact on the receiving societies of interest. Their increased visibility, largely due to their geographic concentration in each country, has generated an expanding body of research on the socioeconomic adaptation of black immigrants.

How well do black immigrants adjust to the U.S. economy? Are they more or less socioeconomically successful than African-Americans? What accounts for observed differences between the two groups? What are the implications of greater immigrant achievement relative to African-Americans for racial inequality in the U.S.? That is, what is the relative importance of race versus ethnicity? These questions have largely defined *previous* research on the economic adaptation of British Caribbean immigrants to the U.S. since the 1960s. The presence of objective differences in labor market outcomes for black Caribbean immigrants and African-Americans lends itself to the issue of racial discrimination. How much can discrimination be blamed for poor African-American outcomes relative to whites if other blacks manage to "make it"? On the other hand, if successful immigrant blacks still do significantly less well than native or immigrant whites, then racial discrimination remains a potential culprit.

Findings have varied with specific dependent variable examined, country of origin of West Indians, and gender. Early studies showed a significant earnings advantage of Caribbean-born males over African-American males (Chiswick, 1982). While some of the earnings advantage was lost in the 1970s so that the earnings of Caribbean men were on par with or lower than those of African-American men (Model, 1991; Butcher, 1994; Dodoo, 1991; Daneshvary and Schwer, 1994), recent studies again show an earnings advantage for West Indian men (Dodoo, 1997), or an earnings advantage for West Indian women and an occupational advantage for West Indian men (Model, 1997).

Explanations of immigrant advantage over African-Americans have included Caribbean cultural superiority, immigrant selectivity, and employer favoritism (see Butcher, 1994; Kalmijn, 1996; Dodoo, 1997). The cultural superiority argument advanced by Sowell and other researchers in the late 1970s attributes black immigrants' success to higher motivation and achievement orientation. This stems from a less extensive period of exposure to slavery conditions that were less harsh than in the U.S., as well as a more favorable post-colonial racial climate in which blacks are the racial majority. This argument of a stronger West Indian work ethic and success orientation as a function of socio-historical differences has not been supported. Many African immigrants also originate in countries that practiced slavery of a kind far less harsh than the dehumanizing version practiced in the New World. Africans also have a strong work ethic and high achievement orientation yet do not have the same advantage of Caribbean immigrants, even with controls for English-speaking ability (Dodoo, 1997).

Another explanation is immigrant selectivity. In general, economic migrants are positively selected relative to their home-country population. While this was true of the predominantly professional class of West Indian immigrants in the 1960s and 1970s, more recent (non-contract) migrants are less selected. Migrant networks have facilitated the easier flow of more working class West Indians to the U.S. so that there is now more diversity of social class and labor market characteristics among Caribbean immigrants (Kasinitz, 1992).

Immigrants are also positively selected relative to segments of the native U.S. population. According to some scholars, given favorable human capital characteristics and time to adjust to the receiving-country economy, West Indian migrants tend to "catch up" or surpass natives after roughly eleven to fifteen years (Chiswick, 1979). Other scholars (Dodoo, 1991a; Dodoo, 1991b; Daneshvary and Schwer, 1994; Butcher, 1994; Kalmijn, 1996), however, point out that while black foreign-born men continue to have higher educational attainment, occupational standing, and employment than U.S.-born black men, they are not able to translate their more advantageous human capital and labor market characteristics into substantially higher earnings. This is because foreign degrees are devalued in the U.S. (Daneshvary and Schwer, 1994). This position is supported in recent research by Dodoo (1997) who finds that the credentials of African immigrants are devalued even more than those of West Indians. More importantly, Dodoo's updated study of immigrant-native earnings differences among men questions the immigrant selectivity argument for West Indians. African immigrants, despite being even more positively selected than West Indian immigrants, achieve only earnings parity with African-Americans, net of other factors. However, Caribbean immigrants have a persistent net earnings advantage relative to African-Americans (Dodoo, 1997). This advantage should have disappeared once immigrant quality was controlled, as occurred with the even more positively selected African immigrants, if selectivity were a valid explanation for West Indian advantage. Dodoo (1997) concludes that a better explanation lies in the differential acceptance of immigrant groups by American society. This explanation lends some support to the argument of employer favoritism for West Indians.

Researchers have also suggested that Caribbean immigrants benefit from favorable employer perceptions of them (Waters, 1994). Some Caribbean immigrants, aware of the stigma attached to blackness in the U.S., distance themselves from African-Americans in the same manner that earlier white and Asian immigrants did. This distancing, as a matter of fact, underlies the social construction of "whiteness" in the U.S. (Olzak, 1992), including the miraculous transformation of "black" European groups such as Italians into "whites." Aware of negative stereotyping of African-Americans and of the fact that white Americans use cues to differentiate them from African-Americans, West Indians apparently play up their heritage to get an edge in the New York labor market. Why their heritage actually gives them this edge has not yet been adequately explained. Model (1997) argues that employers learn to value West Indians more highly than African-Americans from West Indians themselves. However, there is no explanation of why employers would passively believe these foreigners and act on any group-aggrandizement done by West Indian immigrants. Nor is there sufficient consideration of the legacy of historical racism or ongoing institutional discrimination that plagues African-Americans (and blacks, in general, when employers do not care to make any ethnic distinctions).

Recently, scholars (Model and Ladipo, 1996; Model, 1997) have advanced this body of work to compare the labor market outcomes of native and immigrant blacks in a cross-national perspective. How well do the patterns hold up in different national contexts and how well are the current explanations of black immigrant advantage supported? If Caribbean immigrants have better relative outcomes in the U.S. than in other countries as suggested (Model 1997), how adequate are the cultural superiority, immigrant selectivity, and employer favoritism arguments for explaining U.S.-specific findings of West Indian advantage when similar West Indian immigrants reside in other countries of interest?

This issue of the relative importance of race and ethnicity, both in a national and comparative framework, is important. However, almost lost in the debate over whether black ethnic groups have different socioeconomic outcomes and which group does better is the reality that, overall, blacks are not at socioeconomic parity with whites. I advance the scholarship on Caribbean immigrant adaptation by examining the *interaction* of race, immigrant status and education on the occupational attainment of immigrant men *and* women - relative to black native, white native and white immigrant workers - in the national socio-political contexts of the U.S., Canada and England.

Being black in each country carries a social cost, regardless of ethnicity. Education, dubbed a social leveler, is increasingly important for the upward mobility of minorities. Does education differentially mitigate the effect of race or immigrant status on socioeconomic achievement for men and women or across country? I examine occupational attainment rather than earnings because this allows a direct examination of the relative positions of groups in the race-based social hierarchies of each country. The use of a standardized measure of occupational status, the International Socioeconomic Index of Occupations (ISEI), facilitates cross-national comparisons. Also, the British data do not include information on earnings, so the analysis of occupational attainment maximizes comparability of socioeconomic outcomes across country.

In addition to examining the interactive effect of education with race-immigrant status, I explore the role that social structure plays on immigrant achievement. What are the socioeconomic implications for black immigrants of living in countries with varying racial and institutional contexts? What are the implications for non-white immigrants of degree of openness of the social hierarchy in each society?

A BRIEF OVERVIEW OF CARIBBEAN EMIGRATION

Many West Indian nations have a history of post-emancipation emigration that is driven by high unemployment and inadequate economic opportunities at home (Kasinitz, 1992; Palmer, 1995). In this chapter, I examine patterns of Caribbean migration to countries inside of and outside of the Caribbean since the late 1800s and explicate these patterns in terms of formal theories of international migration. In chapter 2, I then explore the implications of the nature of Caribbean migration for the adaptation of West Indians to the economies of the U.S., Canada and England.

Following the abolition of slavery in 1838, plantation owners in Jamaica, major producers of sugar for export, found it hard to employ former slaves. Freed blacks refused to work on plantations that paid a subsistence wage and so they migrated to Trinidad and Guyana, whose plantations had better wage rates. Other islands in the Southern and Eastern Caribbean regularly exchanged workers (Thomas-Hope, 1986; Palmer, 1995). Following the loss of British dominance of the global sugar trade in the 1840s, Caribbean laborers - predominantly from Jamaica and Barbados - migrated to Central America. Foreign investment in Panama, Costa Rica, Mexico, Cuba, Nicaragua and Guatemala created opportunities during the 1840s to early 1900s for unskilled West Indians to work on banana and sugar plantations. These West Indians were also instrumental in building the Panama Canal, railways and other infrastructure related to American investment in Central America and the Hispanic Caribbean (Thomas-Hope, 1986; Kasinitz, 1992; Palmer, 1995). In the 1920s, migration to the these countries was curtailed due to the onset of the Great Depression, completion of major construction projects, and agricultural changes such as crop devastation due to disease (Palmer, 1995).

Migration to the United States began in 1904 following the development of the banana industry by the United Fruit Company, a U.S. corporation. The banana boats used in trade routes between the Caribbean and Atlantic U.S. ports facilitated the development of the tourist industry by providing passenger travel to the Caribbean. Those same banana boats were instrumental in creating counter movements of West Indians to the U.S., which continued unchecked under the immigration quotas established for Britain in the 1920s (Palmer, 1995). While migration to the U.S. ceased temporarily during the Great Depression, labor shortages during and after World War II led to the active recruitment of West Indian labor during the 1940s, predominantly in agriculture. Non-contract West Indian workers of varying skill levels also migrated to U.S. cities to work in service industries from the 1940s to 1952, when controls on West Indian non-contract migration were put in place. Large-scale migration to the U.S. then resumed after the liberalization of immigration policy in 1965 (Palmer, 1995).

Following World War II, Britain also had labor shortages which resulted in active labor recruitment of unskilled and semi-skilled migrants. This stimulated large-scale Caribbean migration to the "mother country" in the 1950s in search of employment opportunities. Initially, these migrants filled low-wage, low-status jobs that natives would not (Owen in Karn, 1997). Mass migration from the Caribbean was deliberately stopped by British immigration policy in 1962. Consequently, significant migrant flows to England shifted to the U.S. and, for the first time, to Canada which also liberalized its immigration policies in the early 1960s.

Overall, migration from the Caribbean has been primarily motivated by high unemployment and underemployment rates as well as poor socioeconomic conditions. Despite some modernization and industrialization, general economic conditions for many countries have not improved significantly since political independence from Britain in the mid-1960s. In fact, these countries have now traded political dependence for economic dependence (Henry, 1994). Most of their economies are still heavily dependent on generating income from tourism and from the cultivation of cash crops for export, a legacy of colonialism. The focus of indebted nations on economic expediency rather than on long-term sustainable development has led to inadequate development of human capital in some economic sectors as well as to significant underutilization of any existing human capital. Therefore, since emancipation, emigration has been highly valued as a means of achieving improved social and economic status (Thomas-Hope, 1996).

CARIBBEAN MIGRATION IN THEORETICAL PERSPECTIVE

•

This general overview of Caribbean migration suggests that several theories of international migration may be useful in understanding immigrant adaptation. These theories are neoclassical economics, new economics of migration, neo-Marxist, world systems, network and migration systems. It is important to recognize that these theories are not mutually exclusive, and each may contribute insights into understanding a particular migration stream or immigrant adaptation.

Neoclassical Economic Theory

Neoclassical economics stresses the importance of geographic differences in wages and employment conditions (see Massey et al., 1993) for migration decision-making. People tend to move toward higher-wage countries from lower-wage countries. At the micro-level, people are assumed to engage in individual cost-benefit analyses and migrate when they can minimize migration costs and maximize the expected net returns to migration, which are calculated based on their human capital investment. This theory is limited in the sense that: 1) it cannot account for some migration flows; 2) it assumes that individuals are rational actors with perfect information about origin and host society economic conditions; and 3) it cannot explain why immigrants (and minorities in general) receive lower returns to their human capital investment than nonimmigrants and white majority workers (Massey et al., 1993; Portes and Zhou, 1992). However, there are some enduring aspects of this theory that are applicable to Caribbean migration. The first is that West Indian migration within the region and to Central America, the Hispanic Caribbean, North America and England did - and still does to some extent - follow the pattern of movement to higher-wage countries with better employment prospects. West Indian labor supplements insufficient domestic labor. The second is that human capital continues to play an important (but not the only) role in the economic adaptation of immigrants.

The New Economics of Migration

The second theoretical approach, the new economics of migration, emphasizes the role that households and families play in migration decision-making. It is a more macro approach than neo-classical economic theory. Migration decisions are made collectively rather than individually to maximize family/household income and minimize or diversify economic risks from certain market conditions or failures (such as loss of crops, lack of insurance markets, or lack of capital for investment). One key issue here is not the lack of wages per se, but that of relative deprivation (see Massey et al., 1993; Portes and Rumbaut 1996). Households are assumed to evaluate their income relative to other households and send workers abroad even when household income is adequate given local standards and cost of living. This theory is useful in explaining why professionals or middle-class families migrate. They perceive a gap in the income they have versus that which they could have if they migrated. Caribbean countries have undergone serious "brain drain" since the 1960s and 1970s because they have "hemorrhaged" layers of workers with professional, technical, engineering and business skills in industries vital for economic development or for even the basic provision of health and public services to local populations (Palmer, 1995).

The emphasis on family decision-making and migration strategies allows closer attention to the ways in which migration is gendered (see Pedraza, 1991). Traditionally, migration has been led by men, and so migration theories have treated women predominantly as tied movers.

However, women have numerically dominated Caribbean migration streams in the last few decades in a trend mirrored by some Asian migration (Pedraza, 1991). This is particularly true of post-1965 migration from the Caribbean. Furthermore, rather than being passive followers, Caribbean women tend to migrate first as part of a family strategy to increase the economic status of their families or households (Foner, 1986). Many make the sacrifice of leaving behind their children and migrating to North America or England. Once they have stabilized their economic position, then they "send for" the rest of their families.

Neo-Marxist/Structural Theories

Neo-Marxist theories add another dimension in helping us understand migration behavior. Rather than focusing on the individual- or household-level migration decision- making process taking place in the country of origin, this approach emphasizes structural factors related to the nature of modern industrial economies in receiving societies. International migration is portrayed as a function of the labor demands of industrial and post-industrial economies. Said labor demands create pull factors for migrants, who are often heavily recruited by business interests in developed nations. One theory subsumed under the generic umbrella of "neo-Marxist theories" is colonization migration. It involves forced migration of labor (African-Americans) as well as the migration of more recent immigrant groups who work under very poor conditions with limited rights and freedoms. These migrants fill labor needs at the very bottom of the occupational hierarchy, working in jobs undesirable to natives (see Portes, 1987; Portes, 1995, Massey et al., 1993). The work of "colonized" migrants is typically restricted to agricultural or other (non-urban) extractive industries (Portes, 1987). Harsh conditions of labor are justified by ideologies of cultural or racial inferiority or else by the economic benefits which accrue to both employers and the members of the receiving society as a whole (Portes, 1987). Some unskilled West Indians are colonized migrants. They are usually signed into short-term contracts for agricultural employees in the U.S. and Canada, and perform grueling labor under harsh conditions, especially in the sugar cane fields of south Florida.

Dual-labor market theory, a variant of the neo-Marxist approach, emphasizes changes in advanced capitalist economies that have led to a bifurcated labor market. Capital-intensive production methods help to keep production costs low and allow employers to respond efficiently to stable consumer demand. However, labor is also needed for optimal response to changes in demand for some goods. Employees who work in capital-intensive industries have stable, well-paying jobs with good benefits, working conditions, and career ladders. Their jobs require higher levels of education and specialized training, often firm-specific. Workers in labor-intensive industries, on the other hand, are less-educated and tend to have unstable, low-skilled jobs with poor wages, status or mobility prospects. Job turnover, underemployment, and unemployment are higher in this second sector of the economy because the workers are more expendable (Sassen, 1995; Massey et al., 1993; Portes, 1987). They are also less likely to be unionized, so they are relatively powerless in relation to capitalists.

Immigrants, especially, immigrant women, are increasingly being recruited into this segment of the economy, as native workers - especially native women - have moved into better jobs or have become unwilling to accept the associated low wages (see Massey et al., 1993). This recruitment into secondary-sector jobs is also an aspect of Caribbean migration to the U.S., Canada and England since the 1950s. In all three countries, West Indian women tend to be concentrated in nursing and lower-status white-collar professions as well as in low-wage (domestic) service jobs. This is in contrast to women from Asia and Latin America, who are disproportionately employed in sweatshops in the textile and food preparation industries. West Indian men, on the other hand, tend to be concentrated in blue-collar occupations such as transportation, communications, and some health care occupations (Foner, 1983; Freeman, 1987; Palmer, 1995; Kasinitz, 1992). Overall, labor recruitment from the Caribbean has been "bifurcated," with the concurrent recruitment of unskilled and professional immigrants (Foner, 1986; Portes and Grosfoguel, 1994).

World Systems Theory

Unlike the previous three theories, world systems theory views migration as a natural consequence of economic globalization. Unlike other theories, it casts specific migration streams in light of colonial and neo-colonial ties between countries. Since the 1600s, capitalist economies have penetrated the national borders of smaller, peripheral societies (less developed nations), creating conditions that are inducive to migration (Massey et al., 1993). Flows of capital to peripheral societies lead to counterflows of labor. Multinational corporations from core societies often build infrastructure to facilitate their economic endeavors and this has the reciprocal effect of enabling local populations to emigrate. Furthermore, multinationals and tourists from core societies expose locals to their culture and way of life. This stimulates specific consumer tastes as well as a general desire among locals to obtain the higher standard of living of core societies. Since the local economies often cannot provide their citizens with adequate employment, especially that needed to increase living standards to those of core societies, emigration is the likely outcome (see Massey et al., 1993).

This theory is particularly applicable to the British Caribbean. Since emancipation, migration within the entire Caribbean basin has been a function of old (British) and new (American) colonial involvement in the British/Hispanic Caribbean as well as Latin America. Migration between the Caribbean and Britain is understandable because of prior colonial ties, since the costs of Caribbean-British migration far surpass the costs of Caribbean-North American migration. Migration to North America is influenced by the strong presence of North American, especially U.S., multinational corporations and to the diffusion of North American culture and ideology to West Indians. So ingrained in Caribbean culture is the expectation of permanent or temporary emigration as well as the desire to have consumer items from abroad that one local Jamaican music artiste dubbed this the phenomenon of the "foreign mind and local body" (Reid, 1986). Such is the cultural legacy of (neo) colonialism.

Network theory

Network theory and the associated concept of cumulative causation have become increasingly important in explaining the perpetuation of international migration. International migrants provide social links between origin and receiving societies. For relatives and friends in their home countries, migrants are a valuable source of information and income that help to defray the costs and risks of migration (see Massey et al., 1993; Boyd, 1989). Migrant networks also operate as employment networks in receiving societies. This is particularly true for women, who utilize family and friendship networks more than men do during both the migration and adaptation processes (Pedraza, 1991). Overtime, as more people migrate, their ties to people in the home country increase the chances of even more emigration by exposing an increasing segment of the origin population to the economic benefits of migrating as well as to new opportunities to move. Because of the cumulative effect of networks on the migration process, in the long-run, migration streams become less selective of the middle-class or others who can afford the initial costs of migrating and become more inclusive of people from the lower and working classes (see Massey et al., 1993). Thus, while migration streams from the Caribbean to North America were dominated by professional and middle-class migrants in the 1960s and 1970s, Caribbean immigrants are now drawn from more diverse social class origins (Kasinitz, 1992; Foner, 1986). Migrant selectivity has declined not only due to the role of migrant networks but also due to increased migration under the family reunification rather than skilled/professional migrant classifications.

Migration Systems Theory

Finally, migration systems theory encompasses the previous theories. It focuses on the ways in which migration flows become stable over time, allowing for the development of specific migration systems. "An international migration system generally includes a core receiving region, which may be a country or group of countries, and a set of specific sending countries that are linked to it by unusually large flows of immigrants" (see Massey et al., 1993; pg. 454). This theoretical approach emphasizes both the micro and macro-level factors that link countries together through the bi-directional movement of people. In addition to economic ties between countries, it acknowledges political, military and social ties as factors underlying migration flows between countries. Migration systems theory also emphasizes networks as the primary link between micro and macro-level factors. Families and households are an important component of networks since they are a socializing agent about migration, as well as the locus of migration decision-making (Boyd, 1989). Macro-level factors are filtered through families who then negotiate responses to these factors (such as immigration policy) as well as to micro-level ones. Given patterns of inter-country relationships and the existence of increasingly large and stable migration flows between Caribbean countries, on the one hand, and North America and Britain on the other, I identify Caribbean migration as occurring within a migration system. This theory orients the cross-national focus of Caribbean immigrant adaptation.

All of these theories explain different aspects of Caribbean emigration and lead us to a basic understanding of who Caribbean immigrants are and why they migrate to the U.S., Canada and England. They also give some insight into how West Indian immigrants get filtered into specific positions in the occupational hierarchies of receiving countries. My focus in this project is to now examine how these immigrants adapt to the economies of receiving societies using occupational status as my dependent variable. While each of the migration theories is important for explaining Caribbean migration, only a subset of these theories is directly applicable to the immigrant adaptation process, the second phase of migration, and *directly testable* given the data under analysis. Chapter two examines implications for immigrant adaptation under models stemming from the neo-classical and neo-Marxist theoretical approaches. Often, the situation of native minorities provides some insight into the long-term mobility prospects of newer non-white immigrants. Therefore, some bridging of the immigration and racial stratification literatures is necessary. Chapters three and four further explore the socio-political context of the U.S., Canada and Britain. Immigration and race relations policies are aspects of the "mode of incorporation" (Portes and Rumbaut, 1996), the context of reception for non-white immigrants that influences their integration into receiving societies. Variations in socio-political contexts may inform national differences in occupational outcomes of Caribbean immigrants. Chapter six compares and contrasts the characteristics of the U.S., Canadian and English samples. Three major sets of comparisons are done: 1) within-country, between race-immigrant group; 2) within-country, between men and women; and 3) between-country (absolute comparisons of groups across country or relative comparisons of difference between groups across country). It is important to note that while the experiences of women are fully examined and are often compared with those of men, this paper does not provide a gendered analysis of immigrant adaptation or work.

Given the background provided in earlier chapters, chapter seven provides the results of multivariate analyses designed to explore the interactive effects of education, race and immigrant status for immigrant men and women. How do non-white immigrants fare in the U.S., Canada and Britain relative to white natives, black immigrants, and white immigrants? Does education differentially counteract the social costs of immigrant status, gender and blackness in receiving societies with race-based social hierarchies?

CHAPTER 2

Theories of Immigrant and Minority-Group Incorporation

The U.S., Canada and Britain now experience tremendous ethnic and racial diversity as a result of a long history of immigration. Scholars are often concerned with who the immigrant groups are, why they migrate, and how they adapt to their new home countries. Immigrant adaptation theories are interlinked with theories of race relations. While the former focus on the incorporation of individuals upon initial contact with a host society, the latter focus on subsequent, established patterns of inter-group relations arising from those initial patterns of incorporation.

NEO-CLASSICAL ECONOMIC THEORY: TRADITIONAL ASSIMILATION THEORIES

The straight-line/functional theory of adaptation (Gordon, 1964) assumes that immigrants as well as ethnic and racial minorities will ultimately give up their culture and blend into mainstream Anglo-Saxon culture, where they will become indistinguishable from the dominant group. According to Gordon (1964), cultural assimilation - the adoption by minority groups of the behaviors, norms, values, attitudes, language, religion, and so on of the dominant group - is prerequisite to the eradication of prejudice and discrimination by the majority group. It is also prerequisite to structural assimilation, the incorporation of minority groups into the structure and social institutions of the host country.

Updated versions of straight-line theory incorporate aspects of neoclassical economics. This theory views the outcomes of immigrants and minorities as the result of the presence or absence of marketable skills rather than the result of cultural assimilation. Under the neo-classical model, immigrants are expected over time to increase their host-country-specific labor force experience and possibly improve their educational qualifications and/or job skills in order to move up the social hierarchy. Even highly educated immigrants are expected to "upgrade" and adapt their education and skills to fit the host-society economy. Thus, both immigrant duration and human capital, which includes English-speaking ability and transferability of job skills, are important for long-term adaptation. To some extent, straight-line theory expects that, relative to natives, immigrants will start off in lower positions in the status hierarchy of receiving societies and work their way up so that their socioeconomic status improves over time (Gordon, 1964). The implication of traditional assimilation theories is that the socioeconomic outcomes for minorities will eventually approximate those of the dominant group as they move up domestic labor queues.

Straight-line assimilation theory has been criticized (for example, Portes (1993)) for its inapplicability to native and immigrant non-whites. Post-1965 immigrants are predominantly from Asia, Latin America and the Caribbean. Relative to native *and* immigrant whites, many have not attained the level of economic success commensurate with their skills or educational qualifications. The credentials of some groups of immigrants are perceived to be inferior by employers in receiving societies and are not as highly rewarded as degrees earned in Europe and North America (for example, Dodoo, 1997). Furthermore, returns to human capital vary among immigrant and minority groups, as well as between men and women. Straight-line theory cannot explain, for example, the disparate economic outcomes between African-Americans and native whites, nor between African-Americans and black Caribbean-Americans. Male Caribbean immigrants have been shown to have higher earnings than African-Americans net of relevant earnings-related characteristics (Dodoo, 1997).

NEO-MARXIST/STRUCTURAL THEORIES

Neo-Marxist Class Conflict

Bolaria and Li (1988) heavily criticize traditional individual-level studies as being devoid of a larger social structural context within which to examine immigrant economic adaptation. Drawing upon the works of scholars such as Lipset and Bendix, Burawoy, Portes, Dahrendorf, and Wallerstein, Bolaria and Li (1988) situate the question of immigrant adaptation within the context of domestic and global labor exploitation. These authors apply a Marxian theoretical framework to the study of historical racial oppression as well as modern-day racism/race relations in the U.S., Canada and Britain. Any question about the economic adaptation of non-white immigrants in the post-industrial economies of these receiving countries must be informed by the nature of the labor exploitation of non-whites under colonial and capitalist economic regimes.

"Relationships of production [are] key to understanding race relations...Race problems begin as labour problems" (Bolaria and Li, 1988; pg. 7). Racism is an outcome of unequal power relationships between dominant and subordinate groups rather than an outcome of cultural misunderstandings. Racism is the resulting ideology used to justify racial domination and exploitation. The use of skin color, rather than ethnicity, to assign groups of people to inferior positions within an economic order began in the 1500s with the British and Spaniards during the era of mercantile capitalism. Slave labor was expropriated - either from captured Africans or indigenous populations of North America, the Caribbean, and South America - to lower the costs of and maximize profits from the expansion of European trade economies. Under colonialism, European expansion into the New World allowed access to rich material resources and the cheap labor of indigenous peoples. Skin color was used to confine groups of people to menial tasks by others who had the power to do so based on their ownership and control of capital (and more advanced weaponry). Different "populations were indentured or enslaved in varying relationships of exploitation" (Bourgeault in Li, 1988; pg. 45) based on their particular usefulness to Europeans and their degree of powerlessness. Ideology based on religious duty to accumulate capital as well as notions of the "uncivilized" nature of non-European people served to justify economic exploitation and reinforce a racial division of labor (Bolaria and Li, 1988).

As mercantilism and colonialism gave way to industrial capitalism, race relations took on a new form. Under capitalism, labor is free because the upswings and downturns of the economy make it more costly for capitalists to maintain an unfree or indentured labor supply. Labor supply by necessity becomes a variable that can be decreased when relative demand is low or increased when relative demand is high for optimal efficiency of production. This is Marx's notion of an "industrial reserve army" of workers, preferably poorly educated, in order to keep down wages and production costs (Bolaria and Li, 1988). Members of the dominant group will be less likely to take on undesirable, poorly paid jobs, so racial minorities tend to fill these slots. When labor demand outweighs supply, immigrant labor - which tends to be drawn disproportionately from the Third World - is by necessity imported to replenish the "reserve army." Over time, the physical and cultural characteristics of subordinate groups become associated with dirty, menial tasks and low social status vis-a-vis the dominant group (Bolaria and Li, 1988).

Importing labor has additional benefits to capitalists, whether labor is highly educated or unskilled. Capitalist economies get the benefit of labor they did not have to produce and pay for. Furthermore, since both the highly and poorly educated non-white immigrants are paid less than their white native-born counterparts, immigrants provide the additional benefit of cheap(er) labor. This is seen as an extension of colonial exploitation of the resources of "Third World" or peripheral countries by core country economies (see Bolaria and Li, 1988).

This Marxist model, for the most part, treats immigrants as a homogenous mass of poorly skilled laborers (now at the mercy of capital). It assumes that immigrants will not improve their human capital in order to achieve mobility across social class boundaries and implies that due to social class barriers, accumulated job experience or human capital will not have significant positive outcomes on the socioeconomic outcomes of immigrants. Furthermore, under this model of (neo) colonial labor exploitation, women undergo "double" and "triple oppression" because of their statuses as women, racial minorities, and immigrants. They are concentrated in occupations at the lowest levels of the occupational hierarchy, particularly in those that are gender-typed and that are part of the secondary sector (Brettell and Simon, 1986). Thus, minority female migrants are expected to do less well than all natives and less well than male migrants, including those in racial minorities.

Other Structural Issues

Other structural theorists take less of a labor-capital conflict approach. They focus more directly on the specific nature of recent changes in post-industrial economies and then on the implications of those changes for minorities and immigrants. They also illuminate non-economic structural issues that impact immigrant adaptation.

First, *economic restructuring* has significantly altered the mobility chances of these newer immigrants and their children by removing many of the urban industrial jobs which prior immigrants used as a stepping stone to upward mobility (Portes and Zhou, 1992; Gans, 1992). Increased immigration since the 1960s has taken place in the context of dramatic changes in the economic structure. In the U.S., the 1970s and 1980s were characterized by 1) de-industrialization, the elimination of labor-intensive jobs in traditional manufacturing or production industries and the movement of heavy manufacturing/production jobs to the South, West and abroad in response to global competition;[2] 2) industrial restructuring, the transition from heavy production or manufacturing industries to high-tech, knowledge-based and service industries as the driving force of the U.S. economy;[3] and 3) decentralization, the movement of production sites from inner city areas to rural or suburban sites (see: Gober, 1993; Frey and Speare, 1992; Portes and Zhou, 1992; Danziger and Gottschalk, 1995; Sassen, 1995). In the early 1990s, there was also corporate restructuring, the elimination of middle management positions and the downsizing of white-collar occupations due to technological changes in information-based industries (see: Gober, 1993; Frey and Speare, 1992; Portes and Zhou, 1992; Danziger and Gottschalk, 1995; Sassen, 1995). Similar economic changes have occurred in Canada and England since the 1970s as they have made parallel transitions (albeit slower and later in the case

·

of Britain) from an industrial to post-industrial economy (Noble, 1981; Esping-Andersen, 1993). Thus, this issue is just as crucial for immigrants in those countries.

These structural changes, in concert with technological changes, have generated greater demand for highly skilled/educated workers, lower demand for low-skill workers in traditional manufacturing jobs, and higher demand for low-skill workers in the service sector. While unemployment has increased among blue-collar and white-collar workers, low-skill workers in traditional industrial occupations have disproportionately experienced rising unemployment and declining wages (Danziger and Gottschalk, 1995; Sassen, 1995). In general, immigrants are over-represented in low-skill, low-wage service and manufacturing (for example, apparel, textiles, food-processing) jobs (Sassen, 1995) thus raising questions about their ability to experience upward social mobility in the long-run without substantial investments in human capital.

Economic restructuring has been particularly detrimental to native minorities in the U.S. and England (Henry, 1994; Sassen, 1995). They, like immigrants, have depended on industrial jobs in cities. With the loss of industrial jobs, the actual movement of industrial jobs overseas, and the growth of jobs in the service sector, minorities have experienced rising unemployment and skill mismatch in the U.S. and England. The skills necessary for employment in manufacturing jobs are not always easily transferable to the service sector. Minorities, blacks in particular, have been adversely affected by the movement of jobs out of cities to suburbs, resulting in spatial mismatch (Wilson, 1996). Without a substantial upgrade in skills, many minorities are increasingly shut out of good jobs in a changing labor market and have become confined to minimum-wage employment in the low-wage service sector (see Portes and Zhou, 1992). So, for both immigrants and native minorities, human capital is important for coping with the changing economic structure.

Second, although differences of socioeconomic outcomes among immigrants stem from differential human capital, including English language ability, *mode of incorporation* (how favorably immigrants are received by the host society in terms of government policy and public opinion, and the presence of co-ethnic communities) differs by immigrant group and affects immigrants' returns to human capital (Portes and

Borocz, 1989; Portes, 1995). For example, European immigrants, especially Northern Europeans, have traditionally been favored in the immigration policies of the U.S., Canada and Britain and now, in the U.S., immigrants of European origin tend to have higher average incomes than both the white U.S.-born population and non-European immigrants (Porter, 1994). Furthermore, *racial discrimination* is an overriding factor in the social mobility trajectory of non-white immigrants. Because of their phenotype, they cannot simply become an invisible part of the mainstream - as did European immigrants - regardless of the duration of time lived in the U.S., Britain, or Canada. Many are subject to overt and institutionalized discrimination which block avenues to economic success. Even when immigrants are from the same region of origin, racial differences in economic outcomes remain (Daneshvary and Schwer, 1994), controlling for human capital and labor market experience. Here, the effect of human capital on economic outcomes for non-white immigrants is influenced by social context.

SEGMENTED ASSIMILATION THEORIES

Some scholars point out that not all immigrants start off at the bottom of the stratification system and work their way up the socioeconomic ladder which, for the most part, has been the traditional pattern of assimilation. Overall, the newer immigrants are more likely than the native population to be *both* undereducated and college educated. Immigrants are also concentrated in the best and the worst occupations (Martin and Midgley, 1994). Diversity of socioeconomic characteristics and reasons for migration (that is, in response to low-skill labor demand, as entrepreneurial/professional class of economic migrants, as political refugees or asylees, and so on) result in *segmented assimilation*, diversity of economic adaptation trajectories of immigrants (Portes and Zhou, 1993; Portes and Rumbaut, 1996). Furthermore, thriving *ethnic enclaves* provide an alternative to participation in the mainstream economy, thus generating debate about the necessity for some immigrants of 1) developing human capital such as English language ability and U.S. (as opposed to foreign) educational credentials or of 2) fully assimilating into the culture of the U.S. mainstream as prerequisite to achieving economic success as suggested by Gordon's (1964) straight-line assimilation theory (see Portes and Zhou, 1993; Portes, 1995; Nee, Sanders and Sernau, 1994; Gilbertson, 1995).

A variant of Portes' segmented assimilation theory is the "ethnic stratification and segmentation" model of immigrant adaptation (Richmond, 1992). This incorporates the impact of structural economic changes on economic opportunities for different segments of the labor market. It also incorporates the notion of "structural pluralism" which recognizes that immigrants enter the labor force of receiving countries at various levels of the social hierarchy, primarily as a function of human capital. However, it further asserts that while there is evidence of structural pluralism, due to forces such as specialization and discrimination, immigrants tend to occupy specific *occupational niches* in the receiving country (see Verma and Basavarajappa, 1989).

These segmentation theories recognize the diversity of social class status and human capital/labor market attributes among recently-arrived immigrants, and make a departure from traditional assimilation and neo-Marxist theories by implying that the human capital and social class assets of immigrants are more important to their short-term economic outcomes than is their immigrant status. The acknowledgment of highly-skilled and highly-educated immigrants allows the examination of the positioning of these immigrants in the social hierarchy of post-industrial societies and of their social mobility trajectories. Furthermore, segmented assimilation models give agency to immigrants, who adapt their skills and characteristics to the opportunity structure of the receiving society by engaging in occupational niching (for example, Gans, 1992) or *entrepreneurship* (Portes and Zhou, 1992).

Overall then, the socioeconomic diversity of newer immigrants as well as mode of incorporation and racial discrimination suggest divergent adaptation strategies and social mobility outcomes that are not accounted for by straight-line assimilation, neo-classical economic or neo-Marxist theories. Differences in socioeconomic success observed between groups of immigrants or between immigrants and natives may be a function of how well groups' individual human capital endowments, influenced by structural factors (mode of incorporation, discrimination), shape their response to the economic context created by restructuring.

In summary and application, I expect that immigrant duration and human capital will have positive effects on immigrants' outcomes under the assimilation model. Consistent with neo-Marxist thought, race will function to place black immigrants at a disadvantage relative to white immigrants and black natives at a disadvantage relative to white natives. Furthermore, "double disadvantage" from a combination of immigrant and race characteristics, will result in poor socioeconomic outcomes of black immigrants relative to white natives. Because of gender discrimination in the labor market, women have lower labor market outcomes than men. By extension, black women should be disadvantaged relative to black men and doubly so relative to white men. In addition, black female immigrants will suffer "triple disadvantage" relative to white native males for having a combination of three exploited statuses. Furthermore, I expect that education will mitigate the effects of immigrant status, race and gender. Will it do so uniformly across country? I anticipate that education will have less of a mitigating effect in countries with a less receptive socio-political context for immigrants and minorities.

CHAPTER 3

West Indian Migration and Socio-Political Context I:
The Racialization of Immigration Policy

· How has "race" directly and indirectly shaped the immigration policies of the U.S., Canada and Britain? All three countries have a history of explicit or implicit race-based exclusion of groups of people from being admitted within national borders. They also have different means of addressing race/ethnic-based discrimination. I track the role of race in admittance policies and explore the social, political and economic contexts surrounding immigration legislation. How have immigration policies reflected the construction of race, and in turn, helped to situate non-whites vis-a-vis whites in the social hierarchy of each country? For the U.S. and Britain in particular, I examine how the construction of national identities - of what being an American or British citizen entailed - contributed to the creation of race-based immigration policies and race-based social hierarchies. However, while racial exclusion was seldom the explicit motivation behind immigration legislation in Canada, Canada did not avoid racial tension and discriminatory social practices. Given inter-country differences in the motivation behind immigration policies, what can we expect for the impact of national race-immigration context for the socioeconomic attainment of black West Indian immigrants? This context informs the mode of incorporation for black immigrants (for example, Portes and Zhou, 1992).

IMMIGRATION POLICY (TRENDS AND CONTEXT), RACE AND NATIONAL IDENTITY.

The United States

Following an open-door trend in immigration from the 1600s, U.S. immigration laws became restrictive in 1875, the beginning of a period of strong negative sentiment towards immigrants. By the 1880s, a significantly increased volume of immigrants, an economic recession, and beliefs about the racial superiority of Anglo-Saxons resulted in organized opposition to the new immigrants and restriction of U.S. immigration laws (Espenshade and Calhoun, 1993). In 1882, Congress passed the Chinese Exclusion Act which "suspended entry of Chinese workers for ten years and barred all foreign-born Chinese from acquiring citizenship" solely on the basis of their race and religion (James and Alexander, 1993; pg. 13). Two more immigration acts were passed in 1885 and 1888 to bar the recruitment of unskilled laborers and deport non-U.S. contract laborers after one year.

Immigration reached its highest rate ever in the early 1900s. Between 1900 and 1910, over six million people came to the U.S., and unlike prior decades of immigration, these new immigrants were predominantly from Southern and Eastern Europe (James and Alexander, 1993). Southern and Eastern Europeans, now classified as "white," were considered *racially* inferior to Northern Europeans. They had darker skin complexions, spoke different languages, and were of different religious backgrounds than Northern Europeans. Southern and Eastern Europeans, like the Chinese and Japanese before them, were subjected to "racial" discrimination and blamed for social ills such as crime. Immigration debates explicitly verbalized the "racial" inferiority of these new immigrants.

Between 1896 and 1917, Congress passed several bills that used literacy requirements to attempt to restrict immigration, culminating in the Immigration Act of 1917. This act was primarily intended to exclude "undesirable" immigrants on the assumption of intellectual inferiority. It also placed an automatic ban on the entrance of Asians, which was not related to literacy. Concerning those "undesirables" who were already in the country, bids were made in Congress to extend Jim Crow racial segregation to them and maintain the racial purity of Caucasians (Carter et al., 1996).

When studies showed that the literacy requirements had failed to limit the number of immigrants or change the predominant countries of origin, the Quota Act of 1921 was passed. This law decreed that the annual number of immigrants admitted from each country would be restricted to 3% of the foreign-born stock of immigrants from each country already represented in the U.S. (James and Alexander, 1993). Total immigration from Europe was limited to 350,000 annually. Since there was a greater stock of Northern and Western Europeans due to immigration beginning in the 1600s, this effectively decreased or completely barred many of the "undesirable" national origin groups. The Quota Act was renewed in 1924 with a national quota set at 2% of the foreign-born stock. In 1927, another renewal lowered the annual European immigration limit to 150,000. The Great Depression of the 1930s lowered immigration and actually led to emigration. Consequently, no major immigration legislation was passed during this decade even though polls taken during this decade showed strong restrictionism (James and Alexander, 1993; Harwood, 1983).

Harwood (1983) viewed the "nativistic restrictionism" of the 1930s as part of the general tone of national isolationism and racial prejudice that existed since the Civil War. Espenshade and Calhoun (1993) link racial and religious prejudice, as well as a belief in Anglo Saxon superiority, to the 1920s bias against immigrants from Southern and Eastern Europe that is reflected in the quota acts passed during that era. Those quota acts remained in effect until 1965. The economic threat posed by the Great Depression also contributed to anti-immigrant sentiment in the 1930s (Harwood, 1983).

During World War II, immigration policy became noticeably less restrictive due to a labor shortage. During the war, the Bracero Program was created with Mexico, Jamaica, Barbados, and British Honduras to allow the temporary immigration of agricultural laborers. This program continued until 1964 when it was officially ended. Following World War II, the Chinese Exclusion Act was repealed, and the foreign wives and children of U.S. servicemen in World War II were allowed entry into the U.S. (James and Alexander, 1993) by the passage of the War Brides' Act in 1946. The Immigration and Nationality Act of 1952 "removed racial barriers to immigration and naturalization" (James and Alexander, 1993; pg. 15). The national origins restrictions were greatly reduced, and among other things, this act introduced U.S. preferences for family members of U.S. citizens and skilled/professional workers. Refugees were openly admitted from Europe in the 1950s, from Cuba in the 1960s, and from Asia in the 1970s following several refugee acts.

The trend toward liberal policy during the 1940s to 1970s was due to America's new role as a superpower with "expanded global responsibilities" (Harwood, 1986; pg. 204). Liberalized immigration policies were part of America's evolving foreign policy obligations, which included a responsibility to be the global defender of democracy and freedom. In addition, America experienced post-World War economic prosperity and a decline in racial and religious prejudice, especially among the highly educated (Harwood, 1986; Espenshade and Calhoun, 1993). In keeping with trends in U.S. government's foreign policy as defender of freedom, the pressure for better race relations at home - followed by the passage of the Civil Rights Act of 1964 - helped to liberalize immigration policy. The national origin biases that restricted particular ethnic, religious and racial groups were removed from immigration policy in 1965.

Neo-restrictionist immigration policies addressing illegal immigration emerged in the late 1980s. The result of this neo-restrictionism was the passage of the 1986 Immigration Reform and Control Act designed to reduce illegal immigration. Employers were forbidden to hire illegal aliens. On the other hand, this immigration act was liberal because it granted amnesty to illegals who had lived continuously in the U.S. since 1982 and allowed them permanent residence rather than calling for their deportation as did 1920s legislation. Immigration policies liberalized again in 1990 with an increase in the annual limit of legal immigrants. Added to family-based and skilled-based preferences was a category that allowed in immigrants of under-represented groups as diversity immigrants (James and Alexander, 1993).

Harwood (1983) argues that neo-restrictionism was due to the increased perception of the public that American culture and way of life were being threatened by high levels of illegal immigration from Mexico. National sovereignty was perceived to be vulnerable to this wave of illegals, who were also linked with concerns about crime. In addition, a downturn in the state of the U.S. economy generated fears about economic security which led to the scapegoating of illegals for the decline in wages and jobs (Harwood, 1986; Espenshade and Calhoun, 1993). However, foreign policy pressures on the U.S. to remain humanitarian and maintain economic and political ties with sending countries, as well as the influence of civil liberties and pro-immigration lobbies, caused immigration policies to remain fairly liberal in the early 1990s.

Canada

Canada's immigration policies of the 1880s, like those of the U.S., placed restrictions on Asian immigration. Both countries had relied on the labor of the Chinese and Japanese to build infrastructure. Canadian immigration legislation of the 1920s also reflected a bias against Southern and Eastern Europeans, whose immigration was heavily restricted. However, unlike the case of the U.S., there never was a verbalization of belief in the superiority of Northern and Western Europeans over other Europeans and non-whites in immigration debates. Canada's exclusionary policies officially reacted to shifts in labor demand and supply or allowed for the statement of geographic or national preferences, never mind their racial implications.

Similar to the trend in the U.S., immigration policy liberalized during the 1940s and 1950s following World War II. High demand for labor led to immigration acts and short-term labor programs that eased restrictions on Southern and Eastern European immigration. Noticeably, non-Europeans were still excluded at this time. A 1952 immigration act allowed for the active recruitment of immigrants to supply labor while at the same time reserving the right to reject individuals or groups on the basis of "...nationality, geographic origin, peculiarity of custom...." and demonstration of a lack of ability to assimilate (Troper, 1993; pg. 262). While this immigration act had the same outcome of excluding "undesirable" groups of people as the U.S.' series of quota acts, again, the excluded groups were never "racialized." In 1956, Canada developed a

Hungarian refugee resettlement program for Cold War exiles, which allowed the admittance of 37,000 Hungarians in one year (Troper, 1993).

In 1961-62, the Canadian economy slowed down and the demand for labor decreased. Active immigrant recruitment by business interests declined (Troper, 1993). At the same time, policy changes during these two years lifted nearly all restrictions on non-European immigration (Richmond, 1990). Immigration inflow, however, was soon restricted by educational and occupational characteristics of immigrants. Legislation passed in 1967 that established a point system based on immigrant social and economic characteristics (Stafford, 1990). In a move toward tighter control, preference was given to immigrants with specific skills, language ability, educational levels and occupation. Those not being sponsored directly by a Canadian citizen had to show that they had pre-arranged employment (Stafford, 1990). On the other hand, legislation in this decade was also liberal. Human rights initiatives, the desire to improve Canada's international image vis-a-vis race relations at home, and Canada's move to establish itself as a leading nation in world affairs and trade all influenced legislation in 1967 (Troper, 1993; Simmons and Keohane, 1992). The 1967 act granted human rights amnesty to illegal immigrants, and all remaining traces of racial and ethnic discrimination were removed from Canadian immigration policy (Troper, 1993).

A 1976 Immigration Act liberalized refugee policy, allowed temporary work permits such as those granted to domestic and farm laborers from the Caribbean, promoted the immigration of economic immigrants, and allowed family reunification. Economic migrants were business people and entrepreneurs with the necessary capital to create jobs. In 1986, this category was expanded to include rich investors such as those who increasingly came from Hong Kong (Stafford, 1990; Richmond, 1990; Marshall, 1987).

In 1987, immigration levels were increased to generate consumer demand for Canadian goods, increase fertility, generate capital investment and create jobs (Stafford, 1990). However, refugee policy became more restrictionist again in 1989 following the passage of two bills limiting refugee admissions. In summary, in the 1980s, family reunification increased in its importance as a preference category for the admission of immigrants (Richmond, 1990).

Canadian policy has paralleled that of the U.S. in that both have adopted similar immigration policies at similar time points in reaction to similar demographic, humanitarian, economic and, to some extent, foreign policy concerns (Richmond, 1990; Troper, 1993). Both countries had racially exclusionary components embedded in their immigration policies until the 1960s. A source of apparent difference is that, despite the reality of racial stereotyping and negative sentiment, race has not been as explicitly tied to immigration policies in Canada as in the U.S. Even Canadian policies which excluded immigrants never "racialized" "undesirable" groups to the extent that the U.S. did by explicitly deeming groups to be racially inferior (see Reitz, 1988). Another interesting difference between Canada and the U.S. is that in the case of the former, very strict immigration controls have been in place since the 1960s, even during subsequent periods of policy liberalization.

England

The British case is different from that of the U.S. and Canada. In the case of the latter, increased immigration in this century took place within a general context of national development and humanitarian concerns. Immigration to the U.S. has been influenced by national development initiatives as well as foreign policy and humanitarian affairs. In contrast, migration to Britain has occurred in the context of colonial relationships.

In the 1940s and 1950s, Britain had an open-door policy. All its colonial subjects were granted automatic status as British citizens by the 1948 British Nationality Act. The motivating factor for this legislation was the desire to foster a sense of community between Britain and its colonies. After WWII, Britain lost to the U.S. its position as the world's superpower, and was "anxious to retain a credible basis for Britain's continued role as a leading world power" (Carter, Green and Halpern, 1996; pg. 142). Extending citizenship to its colonial subjects, some of whom were beginning to foster anti-colonial and nationalistic sentiment, was an attempt to maintain a united front.

However, conservatives became concerned that the offer of citizenship would be taken seriously by colonists who, once they arrived in Britain, would actually be entitled to the same levels of educational and occupational attainment as the British-born (Reitz, 1988; Carter et al., 1996). Conservatives feared that immigration to Britain would increase dramatically once colonists realized what British citizenship entailed. At the very core of British imperialism - and the British identity that stemmed from it - was the notion that Britain was to extend its geographic boundaries outward, not be flooded by "unassimilable" colonists.

The reaction to these fears was the recruitment of immigrant labor specifically from Europe (Carter et al., 1996). European workers were strictly monitored by legislation, unlike colonial workers who were excluded from policy restrictions. A secret Cabinet in Parliament considered strategies to prevent the entrance of non-white colonists (Carter el al, 1966). Immigration of these colonists increased during the 1950s, generating concerns about the threat to the English character of the nation posed by immigrants.

The 1962 Commonwealth Immigrants Act restricted immigration from the colonies by establishing 1) a quota system designed to restrict the total number of immigrants and 2) a voucher system giving preference to immigrants with needed skills or pre-arranged employment. Several other acts of this decade, ending with the 1976 Commonwealth of Immigrants Act, retracted automatic citizenship from colonists and allowed their deportation. The 1976 Act determined that only "patrials" would be true citizens of Britain. "Patrials" were the British-born, or the children and grandchildren of the British-born who resided in either Britain or its colonies (Carter et al., 1996). This Act effectively excluded non-whites from being British because patrials were most likely to be whites. This Act was also heavily criticized as being racist because the volume of immigration of non-white colonists was very low compared to that of white colonists - the Irish. Yet, the Irish were excluded from these immigration acts (Carter et al., 1996; Reitz, 1989).

Even now, British policy is considered very unfriendly towards non-white immigration. In the 1980s, for example, European immigrants accounted for 50-82% of the annual totals of immigrants, while non-white Commonwealth immigrants accounted for an average of a quarter of the immigrant flow in this decade (Richmond, 1990). However, humanitarian concerns in the 1970s to 1980s led to the liberalization of refugee policy, which lessened restrictions on the admission of non-whites.

In summary, the context and motivation behind immigration policy differs most drastically between Britain and North America. "For Britain, non-white immigration occurred in the context of the obligations of a declining imperial power to former colonial territories" (Reitz, 1988; pg. 117). Canada, in contrast, has had a focused, heavily controlled "long-term program of national development" (Reitz, 1988; pg. 117). These contexts have shaped the differential reaction of each country to immigration by non-whites and helped to define the nature of racial interaction.

On the other hand, the U.S. and Britain are similar in that, of the three countries, they have had the most overtly racial immigration policies this century. From 1900-1925 the U.S. passed its most racially exclusionary immigration legislation of this century while the period from 1948 to 1962 marks Britain's shift from an open-door colonial policy to race-based exclusionary immigration policy. Carter, Green and Halpern (1996) link these policy changes to the role of race in the (re)construction of national identities during periods of increased voluntary immigration to the U.S. and Britain, especially of non-whites. Immigration policy becomes the vehicle by which a race-based national identity is formed. The race-based nature of national identity construction during these two periods still determines where immigrants fall in the social hierarchies of each country.

Each nation has used racial categories as the criteria by which to select immigrants for admission to the country. The abstract concept of "race," which is not a biological reality, became specific in its application to people on the basis of complexion, skin color, language, country of origin, and religion (Carter et al., 1996). Thus applied, it became a tool by which to hierarchically rank groups in terms of how well they could "assimilate." Ability to assimilate became a marker of the social desirability of particular immigrant groups, which carried implications for the employment, promotion, earnings and housing prospects of different groups of immigrants (Carter et al., 1996; Reitz, 1989).

In the U.S., the exclusion acts of the 1880s and the quota acts of the 1920s were based on a racialization of everyone not conforming to the Northern/European mold. On the basis of their racialized characteristics, newer immigrants were judged to be far away from what it truly meant to be an "American." They were viewed as incapable of adapting to "American" ways, linked to criminality, and considered threatening to American culture and way of life, including democracy (Carter et al., 1996).

Likewise, in Britain, non-white colonials were also considered to be "unassimilable" to what it meant to be "British." The immigration acts of the 1960s and 1970s that stripped former non-white colonists of automatic British citizenship and imposed skill qualifications sent the message that a true British citizen was white and had certain skill qualifications. The anti-British were non-white immigrants, non-"patrials," who had been linked in 1961 to a host of social ills, such as unemployment, poor housing, venereal disease, and prostitution (Carter et al., 1996; pg. 147). In the case of the non-white colonials, racialization was based on far more visible characteristics such as skin color and hair texture than was the case for Southern and European immigrants in the U.S.

So, while racial prejudice had probably existed on an individual level prior to these two time points, the important observation made by Carter and Halpern (1996) is the role of the state in defining race-based immigration policy and the immigrants' place in the social hierarchy. By making explicit which groups did not fit in enough to be truly "British" or "American," the state "set up" immigrants for state-sanctioned racial discrimination across various societal institutions. This is in addition to discrimination they would have faced in interpersonal daily interactions with the truly " British" or "American."

Carter et al. (1996) excluded Canada from this discussion despite potential similarities to the United States in national identity construction. The literature reviewed mentioned that Canada's immigration policies of the 1880s and 1920s paralleled those of the U.S. While Canada has not had overtly racist immigration policies, its policies prior to the 1960s have been "covertly" racist because of their implications for different groups. Thus, I can only speculate about the exact nature, context and effects of Canadian immigration policies of the 1920s and their effect on the reception of immigrants.

IMMIGRATION, RACE RELATIONS AND SOCIOECONOMIC ATTAINMENT

The racialization of immigration policy and national identity in Britain and the U.S. helped to determine the "place" of groups of immigrants in racially ordered social structures. While Carter et al. (1996) shed light on this process in Britain and the U.S., less has been said about the role of race in shaping national identity and race relations in Canada.

Reitz (1989), however, examines Canada's reception to immigrants in the post-WWII years and contrasts it to that of Britain. Here differences in the context of, or the motivations behind, immigration policy - which make up the institutional structure of immigration - are discussed in terms of their effects on inter-racial competition. It has already been noted that Canada has perceived immigration as a means of national development. Britain, on the other hand, has been rather reluctant to receive immigrants since the 1960s. Consequently, Britain has responded more hostilely to the immigration of non-whites than post-1960s Canada (Reitz, 1989) - or the U.S., presumably, whose policies have often paralleled Canada's. Public opinion data shows that Canadians are more likely to think that immigration is beneficial to the country. The British, in contrast, are most likely to perceive immigrants as a social burden (Reitz, 1989).

Canada's consistently strict control of immigration, especially its preference for skilled workers, professionals, or entrepreneurs, has resulted in a more highly selected stream of immigrants - including non-whites - than the U.S. or Britain (Borjas, 1991; Reitz, 1989). Immigrants in Canada, therefore, have tended to be less residentially and occupationally segregated than those to Britain (Reitz, 1989). Consistent with the fact that non-whites' lower geographic concentration renders them less visible in Canada, the escalation of racial tension into violence has not been as common in Canada (Reitz, 1989; Richmond, 1990). In addition, lower immigrant concentration in "niche" occupations has sparked relatively less inter-ethnic hostility over jobs.

Canada and Britain's immigration policies converged somewhat in the 1970s when Canada adopted restrictive caps on immigrant totals and Britain developed skill-based economic admission criteria (Reitz, 1989).

However, the difference in the reception to and perception of immigrants between the two countries, particularly the absence of overtly racial immigration policies in Canada, has resulted in more benign reactions to non-white immigration in the latter. Race relations, therefore, seem to fare better in Canada relative to Britain.

Given the difference between Canada and Britain in the "institutional structure" of immigration, as well as the race-based national identity construction in Britain and the U.S., what are the implications for socioeconomic attainment of West Indians? Does Canada's lack of overtly racial immigration and general social policy mean that social life is any less hierarchical on the basis of race? Should we expect that immigrants fare better socioeconomically in Canada than in Britain and the U.S.?

While racial problems seem to be less intense in Canada, Canadian society is still racially structured. Similar to Britain and the U.S., access to and attainment of economic resources and rewards is constrained by race. In all three countries, foreign-born black immigrants tend to have worse socioeconomic outcomes in employment and earnings than the white native population (for example, Model, 1991; Kalmijn, 1996; Samuel and Woloski, 1985; Verma and Basavarajappa, 1989; Richmond, 1990). Furthermore, racial hostility, albeit comparatively less intense, is very much a part of the fabric of Canadian social life (for example, Richmond, 1990). Canada, like the U.S. and Britain, therefore is racially discriminatory in terms of the mobility patterns of non-whites vis-a-vis whites, the allocation of power and resources, the use of collective violence against non-whites, and so on (Stanfield, 1991).

The evidence on socioeconomic outcomes for immigrants, given differences and similarities in social and political contexts, reveals for example, that while immigrants to Canada were selective on education and qualifications, the unemployment rate of black immigrants was sometimes as high as that of black immigrants to Britain (Richmond, 1990). Black immigrants to the U.S. on the other hand, despite being less selective relative to Canada's stream, tend to have higher social mobility than those in Canada and Britain (Freeman, 1987; Segal, 1987). The socioeconomic attainment of black immigrants to Britain seems to compare less favorably to that of immigrants to the U.S. and Canada.

DISCUSSION

Overall, the racialization of immigration policies, with its implications for social hierarchies that are race-based, is deleterious for race relations and the position of non-whites vis-a-vis whites. The comparison of Britain and Canada showed that in Canada, which did not have explicitly racial policies, immigrant groups were positioned better vis-a-vis white natives in terms of housing and occupational segregation. Canada's history as a binational society, as well as its current policy of multiculturalism, may foster more pluralistic sentiment and tolerance of diversity as opposed to the more assimilationist stance of the U.S. and Britain.

Britain, which has been overtly racist in immigration policy, tends to have black immigrants who do not compare favorably socioeconomically with black immigrants to other countries. While the U.S. has also been overtly racist, Civil Rights legislation represents an attempt to temper some of the effects of racism on minority outcomes. This may be the primary reason for the better outcomes for black immigrants to the U.S. relative to the other three countries. In contrast to the U.S. civil rights example, Britain has not been so eager to implement policy to combat racism, and where policy has been enacted, enforcement efforts seem minimal (Reitz, 1989). Canada, in keeping with the trend to exclude "race" from social policy, has not passed equal rights legislation. "The absence of a race issue is used to argue that equity legislation is not needed" (Reitz, 1989; pg. 140). Instead, equity legislation has been attached ("piggy-backed") to other measures.

The most interesting observation is that regardless of how racialized immigration and other social policies have been, all three countries show evidence of racism towards non-whites. The presence and enforcement of equal rights or anti-discrimination legislation may be important to the socioeconomic outcomes of black immigrants.

CHAPTER 4

West Indian Migration and Socio-Political Context II:
Race Relations Policy

THE ROLE OF THE STATE: POLITICS AND RACISM

The role of the state in shaping race relations tends to be downplayed for a focus on inter-group or individual-level prejudices and discrimination. Race relations legislation became important for addressing intergroup ethnic/racial inequalities and conflict, particularly those resulting from discrimination against non-whites. Since non-white immigration to the U.S., Canada and Britain increased dramatically since the 1960s, the nature of race relations legislation plays a key role in shaping the socio-political context (mode of incorporation) of Caribbean immigrant adaptation. While immigration scholars (for example, Portes, 1993) have recognized the importance of socio-political context for adaptation, they tend to focus on the receptiveness to immigrants of receiving countries as reflected in the degree of restrictiveness of immigration policy. While all three countries have a history of racism, each has addressed race relations issues differently even though parallels exist in their race legislation. The differences distinguish the specific race-based hierarchy to which non-white immigrants must now adapt. Together, (race-based) immigration and race relations policies help determine the institutional context of immigration, which may have implications for the occupational mobility chances of immigrants.

The United States

The U.S. differs from Britain in that the U.S. has had more contact with far larger populations of racial minorities and number of racial groups within its territories rather than overseas. The U.S. also contrasts with Britain in that "race relations have always been regulated by law whereas in the British Isles, [until 20 years ago], there was in effect no law whatever on the subject" (Claiborne et al., 1983; pg. 4). U.S. law made slavery a valid institution and dictated the terms of white contact with blacks and other non-whites during slavery as well as after Reconstruction. Since law was used to create and legitimate racist structural conditions and social relations, the law was the natural means of dismantling a racially oppressive social system and creating its replacement (Claiborne et al., 1983). Thus, the highly legalistic nature of U.S. society, along with a revolutionary tradition, became advantageous in the struggle for improved race relations and rights of citizenship for racial minorities.

For most of U.S. history, the law functioned to preserve white dominance and privilege. Following the Civil War, attempts to change the status quo were soon deliberately abandoned and replaced with a system of legal apartheid. Lynchings - and to a lesser extent, the complete destruction of thriving, independent black townships and the murder of thousands of the townships' black residents - became more commonplace (Claiborne et al., 1993; Oliver and Shapiro, 1995). Systematic violence against blacks aimed at "teaching the black man 'his place' " (Claiborne et al., 1993; pg. 6) was deemed to be outside of federal power.   The dismantling of this social order did not begin until the mid-1950s when the Supreme Court issued a school desegregation order. Thus began the Court's dismantling of segregation and condemnation of the most violent forms of discrimination although its efforts were initially met with resistance by the white public as well as members of the other branches of government.

Following black political mobilization and activism, a wave of violence against blacks and their supporters in the late 1950s and early 1960s, and America's troubled international image in its role as world superpower, the first Civil Rights Act was signed into law in 1964. This first act dismantled apartheid in most areas of public life. It also legislated against employment discrimination and segregation in institutions receiving federal funds (Claiborne et al., 1983). An Equal Employment Opportunities Commission was established with relatively strong investigative and enforcement powers. Voting rights and discrimination in private housing were later addressed in subsequent civil rights acts. Federal executive orders subsequently ordered the use of "affirmative action" to address the fair employment and treatment of racial and other minorities. These executive orders also allowed for the redress of indirect discrimination and took some of the burden of proof of discrimination away from individual members of the groups protected by law. Immigrants who have been granted legal permission to reside permanently and to work in the U.S. are typically covered by civil rights legislation along with naturalized or U.S.-born citizens.

Despite the controversy surrounding it, Affirmative Action legislation has resulted in substantial improvement in the socioeconomic standing of minority groups. While this legislation has been more rigorously enforced than in Britain, it is still considered to have weak enforcement and monitoring mechanisms. It has also fared better because of the strong judicial support of the Supreme Court (despite recent rulings undermining Affirmative Action). Monetary judgements against defendants are far greater than those allowed in Britain, so that in the U.S., many have learned the lesson that (detectable) discrimination is costly.

In spite of the relative effectiveness of civil rights legislation in the U.S., as well as the much stronger minority political activism and representation at all levels of government, minorities still - like their British counterparts - lack full rights of citizenship. Racial inequalities along all socioeconomic dimensions still abound, and access to equal housing, education and employment opportunities remain limited for many due to the persistence of "governmental, institutional and private-sector discrimination" (Oliver and Shapiro, 1995; pg. 22) which function to keep blacks in a subordinate social position vis-a-vis whites.

Britain

Despite British involvement in slavery in the Americas during the colonial period, Britain differed from the U.S. in that non-whites were largely kept outside of the country's borders. Imperialism functioned to expand the British empire across physical space. It was not expected that exploitation of non-British labor and physical resources would impact the demography of Britain, that colonial British subjects would actually envision going to the "motherland" en masse.

While small black populations existed in coastal towns of Britain for centuries (Solomos, 1989), significant immigration to Britain began after WWII. What obligation did Britain have to its growing population of former colonials, and why not encourage them to return to their origin countries? If they stayed, could they rightfully expect to be treated as English citizens? While anti-white violence has been part of British history long before the post-WWII era, the British had an indecisive "wait and see" approach to "using the law as an instrument of social reform" (Claiborne et al., 1983). This wait-and-see approach extended to race relations. Involved in this indecisiveness was 1) the notion that the law functioned to protect and maintain the status quo, not generate social change and 2) a general resentment by the British of governmental intrusion in private matters - and one's prejudices and discriminatory behavior were considered private (Claiborne et al., 1983). Furthermore, the frank expression of a belief in British (Anglo-Saxon) superiority - based on nationalistic pride from prior colonial dominance over much of Britain's external (predominantly non-white) world - was likely to have a sympathetic response (Claiborne et al., 1983).

British reluctance to legally intervene in racial conflict was overridden in the early 1960s following shocking race riots and particularly high immigration levels. The latter alarmed conservatives who issued dire warnings of race wars and the destruction of British culture and way of life by these "unassimilable" colonials.[4] Rather than trying to address discrimination, the government's response was to pass immigration legislation in 1962 which virtually stopped the immigration of British colonials (Carter et al., 1996; Claiborne et al., 1983).

Due to the recognition that discrimination continued to be a problem, and influenced by the rising political activism of minority groups and their supporters, the government reluctantly issued the Race Relations Act of 1965 which was an adaptation to the British race relations context of the U.S.'s 1964 Civil Rights Act. An important source of difference was the lack of enforcement provisions in the British law. A "Race Relations board with local 'conciliation' committees" (Claiborne et al., 1983; pg. 11) was established to deal with discrimination claims by persuading both parties to settle their differences. Access to legal recourse for plaintiffs was effectively blocked, and the board had very little power over defendants' compliance with their no-discrimination orders. Evidence of persistently high levels of discrimination, anti-immigrant public opinion, and criticisms of the inadequacy of this and subsequent equal rights legislation led to the passage of the 1976 Race Relations Act. Along with recognition of indirect discrimination - discriminatory effects resulting from seemingly non-discriminatory actions or processes - this act expanded the groups to be protected under the act, extended the reach of the law into most public and private spheres of interaction, and established routes to the redress of discrimination (Claiborne et al., 1983). While a new Commission for Racial Equity has been granted the power to investigate complaints and enforce the law, discrimination enforcement remains weak relative to that of the U.S., especially given a lack of strong judicial support of the legislation (Claiborne, 1983; Solomos, 1989). Full rights of citizenship remain elusive for non-whites who still suffer overt as well as institutional discrimination in access to employment, housing and social services (Mason, 1995).

Canada

Canada, like the U.S. and Britain, has had a history of racially-exclusive immigration policy from the late 1800s to the early 1960s. Due to the dominance of British settlers, immigration policy in the late 1800s reflected Britain's in that their ultimate purpose was to exclude non-assimilable immigrants, an initial euphemism for non-Europeans. Canada also shares in common a history of colonial expropriation of black and

Native American labor as well as the legal segregation of black and Native American populations (Walker, 1989). Similar to the U.S., visible minorities - including Asian immigrant labor - were denied full citizenship rights until after WWII, and the law dictated terms of white-nonwhite contact and relations. The law actually created a racially-based caste system in which particular minorities were restricted to specific tasks based on British determination of their economic utility (Walker, 1989). However, for the most part, Canada's discriminatory *race relations* policies were enacted later than similar U.S. policies and lasted for shorter periods of time.

Racist WWII atrocities influenced greater reception of white Canadians to minority groups' efforts to obtain citizenship rights. A plan to intern Japanese-Canadians in camps in 1942 fueled anti-Nazism protest and lead to the passage in 1946 of the first Citizenship Act. This act changed the meaning of "Canadian" to a more inclusive one by legislating an end to legal distinctions between Canadians on racial or other grounds (Walker, 1989; pg. 10). "Human rights" became a valid term, and laws which enforced racial disadvantages began to be repealed, especially because they contradicted Canada's interests of becoming a world leader. Key components of this role involved the support of democratic ideals and the promotion of basic rights.

Despite Canada's liberal international policies, the recognition that racial discrimination was wrong did not necessarily lead to the acknowledgment that Canadians actually practiced it (Walker, 1989). Incidences of blatant discrimination were addressed with attempts to enlighten rather than to punish. Fair Employment Practices and Fair Accommodations Practices Acts were passed in 1951 and 1954 to target specific types of racial discrimination. However, like the first British Race Relations Act, Canada's anti-discrimination legislation so far did not allow compensation for discrimination and was practically unenforceable (Walker, 1989). In 1960, a federal Bill of Rights was passed which reiterated that racial discrimination was contrary to public policy.

Finally, due to international and domestic pressures to end continued discrimination, anti-discrimination laws were consolidated into the 1962 Human Rights Codes. Full-time commissions were established to investigate complaints, but the conciliatory nature of the laws was changed over the course of a few years as more anti-segregation and discrimination amendments were passed. The 1970s, however, saw a resurgence in racially-motivated hostility and crime because of the presence of dramatically increased non-white immigrant populations, whose high qualifications gave them access to spheres of social life typically closed to non-whites (Walker, 1989). The Human Rights Codes were powerless to address this new race relations problem and the federal government turned to policies of multiculturalism.

A 1971 multicultural policy was adopted to "preserve the language and heritage of all ethnic groups and removing social obstacles towards equality" (Li, 1990; pg. 14). Federal funds were allocated for language and culture maintenance, and social, cultural and racial harmony were promoted. This policy became law in the Canadian Multiculturalism Act of 1988. This act, in addition, sought to promote cross-cultural understandings, "...reduce discrimination, and accelerate institutional change to reflect Canada's multicultural character" (Elliott and Fleras, 1990; pg. 65). It emphasized the rights of individuals to identify with their chosen cultural heritage "yet retain access to equal involvement in Canadian life" (Elliott and Fleras, 1990; pg. 65).

Critics of this policy claim that it really has not adequately addressed racism and discrimination. Rather, multiculturalism - through its funding of multicultural activities - is really a convenient way for the state to control ethnic associations since funded associations must comply with certain governmental multicultural criteria. The policy allows the state to control and restructure race and ethnic relations and the power and resource bases of ethnic and racial groups (Li, 1990). In any case, the policy is an attempt to embrace all cultures on their own terms, or with mutual respect, in contrast to the assimilationist stance of England and the U.S. It provides a significant political break from previous discriminatory policies that often paralleled U.S. policies.

The differences in socio-political climate may impact the course of immigrant adaptation. As they become incorporated into the U.S., Canadian and British societies, non-white immigrants have to contend with racially biased social institutions. Britain has weak enforcement of equal rights legislation so that non-white immigrants to Britain may have poorer outcomes than non-white immigrants to countries with more rigorous monitoring and enforcement.   In the U.S., relatively more aggressive monitoring and enforcement can become deterrents to discrimination in the first place. `Immigrants benefit from the same anti-discrimination programs as natives and, given time in the U.S., they become socialized into a culture of rights which legally protects minorities from overt job or other discrimination.   With Canada, it is not clear whether multicultural policy and the funds allocated for multiculturalism have succeeded in producing change in the nature of social structures which have perpetuated occupation-based racial inequality.

In summary, the socio-political context of receiving countries, as defined by race relations, immigration policies and race relations policies, is conceptualized as part of the "mode of incorporation" for non-white immigrants.   To what extent do national differences in socio-political context inform between-country differences in the occupational outcomes of West Indians?   Researchers tend to focus on West Indians because they seek to examine the relative effect of race and ethnicity on socioeconomic outcomes.   However, despite ethnic differences in outcomes among blacks, *racial* inequality remains a stark reality.   I draw on the neo-classical and neo-Marxist theoretical approaches to examine whether education differentially mitigates the effect of race and immigrant status on occupational attainment for men and women.   What are the implications of these associations for the openness of the social hierarchy in each society? What are the implications of degree of openness for non-white immigrants?

CHAPTER 5

Data and Methods

In the U.S., Canada and England, Caribbean immigrants are an urban population. Roughly half of Caribbean immigrants to the U.S. live in the New York City metropolitan area. The other half is highly concentrated in Miami, Florida; Hartford, Connecticut; Boston, Massachusetts; and Newark, New Jersey (Kasinitz, 1992; Palmer, 1995; Kalmijn, 1996). In Canada, over half live in Toronto, while others live in metropolitan areas such as Montreal and Ottawa-Hull (Statistics Canada, 1992b). In England, Caribbean immigrants are concentrated in metropolitan areas in the Southeast, particularly in the London area, and in West Midlands County, which has a strong manufacturing economic base (Karn, 1997).

This concentration of immigrants in particular urban areas led to the selection of specific metropolitan areas for study. One benefit of this sampling strategy is that, since both the native and immigrant populations have been selected from the same metropolitan areas, immigrants have a focused comparison group (Ko and Clogg, 1986). This controls for heterogeneity among the native groups, such as rural-urban differences, that would undermine the validity of immigrant-native comparisons.

DATA

The United States

Since the West Indian population is highly concentrated, I examine only those areas with a significant Caribbean population base. Thirty (30) metropolitan statistical areas (MSAs) were selected based on a minimum sample size requirement of 60 black Caribbean men and women in each area. In order to control for variations in the characteristics of MSA, I created a multilevel data file by attaching geographic data from the 1990 U.S. Census' Summary Tape File 3A (STF) to the 1990 5% Public Use Microdata file (PUMS).

The PUMS sample drawn for analysis is a representative sub-sample of black and white native and foreign-born individuals from the non-institutionalized, civilian, non-Hispanic population aged 16-65. Excluded from this study are people born in U.S. outlying areas and territories, as well as those born abroad to American parents. Because Caribbean immigrants are native speakers of English, the white foreign-born sample was restricted to immigrants who are also native speakers of English or who speak English well or very well. English-speaking ability is a primary determinant of immigrant socioeconomic attainment in mainstream labor markets (see, for example, Kalmijn 1996) so the immigrant groups were equalized on this variable for optimal comparability.[5] In order to have an approximate sample size of 10,000 for each group, white natives were sub-sampled to 0.8 percent of their original sample size, white immigrants to 10 percent, black natives to 4 percent, and black immigrants (Caribbean-born) to 51 percent.[6]

England

The 1991 Census of Great Britain provides both individual and summary level data. Similar to the U.S. census, basic demographic information was obtained from the general population, from which 10% of people answered more detailed open-ended questions. The 2% Individual Sample of Anonymised Records (SAR) was drawn from this coded 10% data. To the 2% individual-level file I attached data from the 1991 Local Base Statistics (LBS) summary file which contains detailed geographic socioeconomic information. The same criterion of a minimum population of 60 Caribbean blacks was applied to the British data. Because of the pattern of concentration of Caribbean immigrants in Great Britain, 22 of 278 local areas in England were selected for analysis.

From the 2% Individual Sample of Anonymised Records (SAR) data, I drew a representative subsample of the non-institutionalized, civilian population of native-born and immigrant whites and West Indians aged 16 to 65. Unfortunately, the U.K. census data have no information about the English-speaking ability of immigrants, thus the sample of white immigrants may vary widely on English ability. Given their over-representation in the 2% data, white natives were sub-sampled to 5 percent and white immigrants to 33 percent of their original sample size so that there were 2860 white natives, 2661 white immigrants, 2731 black U.K.-born West Indians, and 2477 black Caribbean-born immigrants.[7] There was no further sub-sampling of black natives or immigrants given their already small sample size. A caveat to the race information is that West Indian countries are racially heterogeneous, some countries more than others. It is possible that England may classify some of the non-black, non-white racial groups from the Caribbean (mixed, East Indian, Chinese, Syrian, and so on) as "black" based on place of birth data.

Canada

The Canadian data used in this analysis are from the 1991 3% Census Public Use Microdata File (PUMF) and the 1991 Census Basic Summary Tables (BSTs). The individual microdata sample was selected from a one-fifth sample of the general population who answered a detailed census questionnaire (Statistics Canada, 1994). I attached socioeconomic information about Canadian census metropolitan areas (CMAs) from the 1991 BSTs to the individual PUMF data file. The selection of CMAs which had at least 60 Caribbean immigrants yielded only seven (7) viable geographic areas.

I drew a representative sample of the non-institutionalized, English-speaking population of black and white immigrants and natives aged 16-65. The Canadian data did not allow for the separation of the civilian from the military population. Because of their greater representation in the census files, white natives were sub-sampled to 4% and white immigrants to 32% of their original sample size for final samples of: white native 3279, white foreign-born 3467, black native 1635, and black Caribbean-born 3436.[8] Black groups were not sub-sampled in the 3% data due to fairly small sample sizes.

SAMPLE SELECTIVITY

Of interest in this study is the occupational attainment of black immigrants relative to white natives, white immigrants and black natives (where applicable). However, some individuals do not have information on occupational attainment because they are absent from the labor force. Analyses of occupational attainment may yield biased parameter estimates because these individuals are excluded from the labor force in a systematic (nonrandom) manner (Heckman, 1979). Sample selection on the dependent variable needs to be accounted for in regression models by an additional variable. Without a correction for sample selection, the effects of the independent variables in a model are confounded with the disturbance term (Berk, 1983); in effect, a specification error occurs in which the independent variables are correlated with the error term.

I use a two-stage sample selection correction method similar to Heckman's (1979). For each country, I first estimate a logistic regression model of labor force participation to determine the likelihood of being in the labor force. I then transform the predicted logit into a correction term, lambda (see Blau, 1985).[9] This term is then inserted into the models of occupational attainment, which are run only on individuals with non-missing values for the occupational status score.

While the variables used in the logistic labor force participation models may vary somewhat by country, common key variables are included in the selection analyses for each country. They are defined in Table 5.1. Gender is an important selection factor since women tend to have lower labor force participation relative to men. Furthermore, married women have historically been less likely to participate in the labor force than other women although their labor force participation has increased over the last thirty years (see Rindfuss, Brewster and Kavee, 1996). Also, married women having only dependent children below the age of six have traditionally been less likely than those with school-age children to be in the labor force. Thus, marital status and the presence of only pre-school children (where available; see notes b and d in Table 5.1) are included as predictors of labor force participation. They are expected to lower the likelihood of labor force participation for women.

Because I am interested in comparing labor market outcomes for black and white immigrants and natives, race-immigrant status is a key independent variable in the labor force participation models. England and Canada do not have as established a native black population as does the U.S. due to historical factors. While both countries have accepted black immigrants and have had black residents for many years, the bulk of their black population arrived since the 1960s. Therefore, in both these countries, the native black population comprises predominantly second-generation black immigrants. This is in contrast to the United States in which "native black" for the most part refers to African-Americans, a more established black ethnic group with its own unique historical experiences in the U.S.

Age, educational attainment, disability status (U.S. and U.K.), duration time in the receiving country for immigrants (U.S. and Canada) and school attendance are also included as predictors of labor force participation (see Kahn and Whittington, 1996; Krishnan, 1992; Wright and Hinde, 1991). Qualifications are used to gauge educational attainment rather than measures of "highest grade attended" (Canada), "highest grade completed" (U.S.), or "number of years in school." This allows for data compatibility with England. Work disability is defined in the U.S. census as a physical or mental health condition lasting six or more months which limited or prevented the kind or amount of work a person could do (Bureau of the Census, 1992b). The U.K. uses the term "limiting long-term illness" to refer to disability. This is defined as any long-term illness, health problem, or handicap which limits daily activities or the work one can do (OPCS, 1992).

Some scholars have called into question the validity of regression outcomes gĕnerated by models with Heckman's sample selection correction. Often, attempts to correct selection bias result in even greater bias since the predictors in both the first- and second-stage equations are identical (Berk, 1983; Stolzenberg and Relles, 1997). Thus the correction term is highly correlated with the independent variables in the second-stage model. In order to avoid such a bias, where predictors of labor force participation overlap with predictors of occupational attainment, I vary the specification of those predictors when possible. For example, educational attainment is predictive of both labor force attachment and occupational outcomes. It is measured by a dummy variable for post-high-school education in stage 1 models of labor force participation and by dummies for credentials or qualifications in stage 2 models of occupational attainment.

MODEL: ANALYZING OCCUPATIONAL STATUS

" The division of labor is the kernel of social inequality, and occupation...is the main dimension of social stratification... "
(Ganzeboom and Treiman, 1996).

Dependent Variable

Work roles are the most important adult roles outside of family/household roles. The jobs which people hold give us clues about people's 1) labor market characteristics such as skill levels or educational attainment 2) social class background and 3) current and future socioeconomic standing (Hauser and Warren, 1997). Thus, measuring occupational status has been crucial to social stratification research. As the labor markets in industrialized nations have diversified along racial, ethnic and gender lines, occupational status scales have become instrumental in gauging the social status of one group relative to another.

While various measures of occupational status exist, I use the International Socioeconomic Index (ISEI) of Occupations developed by Ganzeboom and Treiman (1996). It is based on the Socioeconomic Index of Occupations (SEI) which was first developed by Duncan (1961). Updated versions of the SEI have been constructed for national and cross-national research (for example, Hauser and Warren, 1997; Ganzeboom and Treiman, 1996; Nakao and Treas, 1994; Ganzeboom, De Graaf and Treiman, 1992; Stevens and Featherman, 1981). In general, prestige scales are first constructed from the results of nationally representative social surveys which ask respondents to make judgements about the status of occupations (see Duncan, 1961; Nakao and Treas, 1994). Then, the prestige scores of occupational titles are regressed on the age-standardized characteristics (usually, average income and average educational attainment) of the incumbents of matching U.S. Census occupational categories (Ganzeboom, De Graaf, and Treiman, 1992; pg. 6). SEI scores are ultimately derived from the resulting regression equation. Thus, SEI scores are weighted averages of occupational education and income (Hauser and Warren, 1997) which are mapped to occupational classifications. Rather than being a subjective measure of occupational status, the socioeconomic index of occupations - divorced from prestige scores - is an objective measure which taps the dimensions of occupations that are important for social mobility.[10]

The comparative analyses involving the U.S., Canada and England use the Standard International Socioeconomic Index of Occupations (ISEI) to measure occupational standing. The ISEI is conceptually close to the SEI but there are some notable differences. Like the SEI, the ISEI is a weighted sum of the age-standardized socioeconomic characteristics of occupational incumbents but it is based on the 1988 International Standard Classification of Occupations (ISCO-88) rather than on a national occupational classification (Ganzeboom and Treiman, 1996). This allows for cross-national comparisons of occupational attainment and mobility. Furthermore, while the SEI scale a) takes prestige scores as its point of departure and then b) makes use of weights for education and income which "maximize their joint correlation with prestige" (Ganzeboom, De Graaf and Treiman, 1992; pg. 10), the ISEI scale is a) derived from SEI scores rather than prestige scores and b) uses weights which maximize the intervening position of occupation between education and income. With the use of 1) path models involving age, education, SEI scores for occupational categories, and income and 2) a new algorithm for computing ISEI scores from regression results, Ganzeboom et al. (1992) create ISEI scale scores that minimize the direct effect of education on income. Instead, ISEI scores emphasize the correlation of education with occupation and of occupation with income (see Ganzeboom, De Graaf, and Treiman, 1992). Thus conceptually, more than the SEI, the ISEI taps the attributes of occupations which convert education (primary personal resource) into income (primary personal reward) (Ganzeboom, De Graaf and Treiman, 1992).

Independent Variables

Studies (Chiswick, 1982; Daneshvary and Schwer, 1994; Poston, 1994; Borjas, 1990; Dodoo, 1991b; Kalmijn, 1996) show that human capital is a primary determinant of labor market outcomes. For immigrants, human capital includes not only educational attainment, but also English-speaking ability and host-country-specific labor market experience (Dodoo, 1997). Married men have better labor market outcomes relative to non-married men so marital status is another key variable. Age influences the life cycle patterns of labor force activity and economic outcomes (Poston, 1994). In the U.S., public sector employment is a major avenue of economic success for blacks, while self-employment is an alternate route to success for minorities and nonwhite immigrants who have been shut out of mainstream jobs due to discrimination or lack of adequate qualifications (Portes, 1995; Waldinger, 1997). Self-employment is also an alternate route to economic assimilation for immigrants in enclave economies whose support networks provide them with access to labor and capital. Gender differences in labor market outcomes are endemic in post-industrial societies (King, 1995; Model and Ladipo, 1996; Reskin, 1990) due to gender discrimination in the allocation and rewarding of jobs. These key factors are included in models of occupational attainment in each country. They are defined in Table 5.2.

OLS regressions were run separately for each country. An individual's chance for economic success is determined not only by individual-level characteristics, but also by the constraints and opportunities present in the local community in which he/she lives and works. Local labor market areas have social and economic characteristics, such as educational opportunities and types of employment, that create a particular opportunity structure (Tickamyer, 1992). Studies have shown that high minority concentration in an area is linked to poorer socioeconomic outcomes for minorities relative to whites. For example, Tootle and Tigges (1993) and Semyonov, Hoyt and Scott (1984) show that due to inter-racial labor market competition, higher black concentration in U.S. Southern labor market areas is associated with higher black unemployment and lower chances for blacks of occupying upper-level white-collar and professional jobs. Racial composition of labor market areas thus helps to define a constraining opportunity structure for individual outcomes.

Given that certain labor market characteristics may affect individual-level outcomes, OLS regressions include controls for characteristics of metropolitan areas that may distort the effects of individual-level predictors. The control variables in Table 5.2 tap spatial inequality. They are measures of industrial structure, labor market supply and demand, and racial composition. There is an additional place control for specific geographical patterns of concentration among immigrants.

Table 5.1: Variables Used in the Analyses of Labor Force Participation

Variable	Description
Dependent Variable	
LFORCE	1=In the labor force; 0=Otherwise
Independent Variables	
Age (years)	Age and Age-squared
Gender	1=Male; 0=Female
Race-Immigrant status	Black Caribbean-born; White foreign-born; Black native (born in the U.S. or England or Canada); White native - reference
Immigrant Duration [a] (U.S. and Canada)	11 or more years; 0-10 years; native - reference
Dependent children [b]	U.S. and Canada: presence of own children below age 6 only (for women); U.K.: presence of dependent children.
School enrollment	1= Attending school; 0=Otherwise
Disability status [c] (U.S. and U.K.)	1=Long-term disability which limits or prevents work; 0=Otherwise
Educational Attainment	1=Post high school education; 0=Otherwise
Marital status [d]	1=Married; 0=Other

[a] The U.K. Census data lack duration information.

[b] In the U.S., this variable means: presence in the household of own children less than 6 years old only. In Canada, this variable means: presence in the Census family (which can be a subset of the household unit) of own children less than 6 years old only. In both countries, this information is coded only for women aged 15 and over. In the U.K., this variable means: presence in the household unit of dependent children. No information is available about the age of dependent children.

[c] No information about disability is available in the Canadian census.

[d] In England, the "married" category may contain separated people. No distinction is made between "married, living together" and "married, separated."

58

Table 5.2: Variables Used in the Analyses of Occupational Attainment

Variable	Description
Dependent Variable	
Occupational ISEI score	International Socioeconomic Index of Occupations (Ganzeboom and Treiman, 1996)
Independent Variables	
Individual Immigrant Adaptation Variables	
Race-Immigrant status	Black Caribbean-born; White foreign-born; Black native (born in the U.S. or Canada or England); White native (reference)
Gender	1=Male; 0=Female
Age (years)	Age and Age-squared, centered
Educational Attainment (coded to British data)	Highest level of qualification: No post-high school qualification (reference); post-high school diploma/certificate but no university degree; B.A. or "first. degree" or equiv.; post-B.A. degree
Duration of time in host country (U.S. and Canada only)	Number of years since entry into host country (categorical): Natives - ref.; 0-10 yrs; 11-20 yrs; more than 20 yrs.
Marital status	1=Married; 0=Otherwise
Class of worker	U.S.: Self-employed; Public sector; private sector - reference U.K. and Canada: 1=Self-employed; 0=Otherwise
School attendance	1= Attending school; 0=Otherwise

Table 5.2 continued: Variables Used in the Analyses of Occupational
Attainment

Variable	Description
Structural Controls: **Labor Market Area** **characteristics**	
Economic Base	% of the population employed in high-wage service industries.[11]
Quality of labor supply	% of population with a B.A. degree or higher
Labor demand	% of population unemployed
Entrepreneurship	% of population self-employed (where available)
Black concentration	% of population black
Immigrant concentration	% of population foreign-born
Place/Region	U.S.: Northeast, Midwest, West, South (reference)
	U.K.: Southeast, West Midlands, Other (reference)
	Canada: 1=Toronto; 0=Otherwise (no region variable available)

60

CHAPTER 6
Preliminary Analyses

SAMPLE SELECTION

In each country, samples were drawn of the non-institutionalized population of black and white native and foreign-born individuals aged 16-65. Table 6.1 illustrates that in all three countries, working-aged men have significantly higher rates of labor force participation than their female counterparts. This is true for each race-immigrant group with the exception of black natives in Canada, where men's and women's participation rates are roughly equivalent. In North America, the gender difference between blacks is much smaller than between whites, mainly because black females have higher labor force participation rates than white females in general. In contrast, the U.K. gender difference in labor force attachment seems consistently large across race-immigrant group.

Within gender, patterns of race-immigrant differences in labor force attachment vary across country. Among U.S. men, all whites have significantly higher labor force participation than all blacks in this study. However, black Caribbean immigrants have far greater labor force attachment than black natives. The opposite is true for white immigrants and white natives. The patterns for U.S. women reveal that Caribbean immigrants have higher labor force participation not only relative to black natives but also relative to all whites. White immigrants, on the other hand, have the lowest labor force attachment of all groups. As is the case with men, black natives participate in the labor force at a lower rate than white natives.

In Canada, black native men have significantly lower labor force attachment than all other males, a pattern also seen in the United States. Caribbean immigrants have the same level of labor force attachment as white natives, while white immigrants have an exceptionally high rate of participation in the labor force. The women are interesting because of the similarity in their labor force attachment. As in the U.S., Caribbean immigrant women have significantly higher labor force participation than all other women. However, the latter do not differ significantly among themselves in participation rates.

The U.K. patterns of labor force participation are even more dissimilar than those in North America. Black natives, Caribbean immigrants and white natives do not have significantly different levels of labor force attachment. Furthermore, white immigrants have significantly lower labor force participation than all other groups (as seen for U.S. women). These patterns are identical among both men and women.

What are some of the factors that influence labor force participation? For each country, I estimated a logit model of labor force participation using the variables defined in Table 5.1. Table 6.2 reveals that being male directly increases one's chances of labor force participation in the U.S. and England. In all three countries, gender interacts with marital status. The main effect of marriage is to lower the likelihood of labor force participation. However, the interaction effect reveals that in each country, while marriage negatively affects women's chances of being in the labor force, it actually increases men's likelihood of labor force participation. On average, school attendance, dependent children, and disability (U.S. and U.K.) decrease the likelihood of labor force participation while post-secondary education increases it.

In North America, the data allow the assessment of the effect of immigrant status by duration. The U.S. results shown in Table 6.2 reveal that black natives have significantly lower likelihood of labor force participation relative to white natives. So do white immigrants. Furthermore, white immigrants who arrived to the U.S. between 1980 and 1990 are even less likely than more settled ones to be in the labor force. In contrast to white immigrants and black natives, black immigrants who have been in the U.S. for over ten years are more likely than white natives to be in the labor force, net of other factors. Recent black immigrant arrivals are no more or less likely than white natives to be in the labor force. The Canadian results in column 3 are similar to those of the U.S. in that black natives and less settled white immigrants have lower likelihood of labor force participation than white natives, net of other factors. However, the patterns diverge in that recently-arrived black immigrants are actually less likely than white natives to be in the labor force. Furthermore, immigrants of either race who have been in Canada for more than ten years are not significantly different from white natives in likelihood of labor force participation.

In contrast to those in North America, black natives in the U.K. are no more or less likely than their white counterparts to be in the labor force, net of other factors. In the absence of duration data, black immigrants on average are more likely to be in the labor force than white natives. On the other hand, white immigrants have lower likelihood of labor force participation.

Tables 6.3, 6.4, and 6.5 contain gender-specific logistic regressions of labor force participation. The effects of age, marital status, dependent children, school enrollment, disability, and post-secondary education are consistent with those results reported in Table 6.2. This is true in each country with one exception. In the U.K. (Table 6.5), while post secondary education increases the likelihood of labor force participation among women, it has no significant effect for men, net of other factors. In addition, while women's chances of labor force participation are negatively effected by the presence of dependent children, men's labor force participation occurs independently of children.

There are a few additional differences in the likelihood of labor force participation by gender. In the U.S. (Table 6.3), while black native men are less likely than white native men to be in the labor force, black native women have the same likelihood as white native women, net of other factors. Furthermore, among immigrant men, duration is more predictive of labor force participation than race, in a pattern consistent with assimilation. Recently-arrived immigrant males of either race are significantly less likely to be in the labor force than white native men. On the other hand, more settled immigrant males of either race are not significantly different in likelihood of labor force participation relative to white native men (at alpha=.05). The patterns for white immigrant women are also consistent with assimilation. Although all white immigrant women have lower likelihood of labor force participation relative to white native women, there is a pattern towards immigrant-native similarity as duration increases. Black immigrant women, on other hand, have greater likelihood of labor force participation than white natives and the difference only increases with duration. So for women, all natives have the same likelihood of labor force participation regardless of race. However, immigrant effects are distinctly race-specific.

In Canada (Table 6.4), the partial effects of race-immigrant status differ by gender as well. As in the U.S., black native men are less likely to be in the labor force relative to white natives while there is no significant difference in likelihood between black native and white native women. Among men, there is no significant difference in likelihood of participation between white immigrants and white natives, net of other factors. In a pattern consistent with assimilation, black immigrants males in Canada for ten years or less have lower likelihood of labor force participation than white native males.. More settled black immigrants do not differ significantly from white natives. Among white immigrant women, an assimilation pattern is also evident. Shorter duration lowers the likelihood of labor force participation relative to white natives while longer duration eliminates significant difference between white immigrant and white native women. However, black immigrant women of either long or short duration, like black native women, do not differ significantly from white native women, net of other factors.

In the U.K. (Table 6.5), in the absence of duration data, white immigrant males are significantly less likely to participate in the labor force, net of other factors. White immigrant women, on the other hand, do not differ significantly from their native counterparts in likelihood of labor force participation. Caribbean men - native or immigrant - are no more or less likely to participate in the labor force than white native men. This pattern is consistent with that for native Caribbean women relative to native white women. However, as in the U.S., black immigrant women have significantly higher likelihood of labor force participation relative to white native women.

The estimated logits from the labor force participation regression models above were used to calculate sample selection correction terms, both general and gender-specific. These terms were then entered into models of occupational attainment. Excluded from the remainder of analyses are individuals without an occupational classification or ISEI score.

DESCRIPTIVE ANALYSES

Occupational Attainment

Tables 6.6 and 6.7 show occupational distributions and mean occupational status scores for women and men, respectively, in each country. How do race-immigrant groups vary within country by gender? How similar are patterns of inequality across country? Overall, women are concentrated in professional specialty and technical, administrative support, sales, and service occupations (Table 6.6). Black immigrant women are particularly concentrated in service jobs in the U.S. and England, while those in Canada are most highly concentrated in lower-status white-collar work. In all three countries, professional specialty/technical or administrative support occupations are the second most common source of employment for Caribbean immigrants. In England and the U.S., relative to other groups of women, West Indians have the lowest representation in executive, managerial and administrative occupations. This under-representation is particularly stark in England where only 4% of West Indian women are employed in top occupations. Roughly 8 to 10% of black immigrant and native women in the U.S. and Canada, and 8% of black native women in England, are employed in these occupations. In contrast to black immigrant women, black native women are most highly concentrated in administrative support positions in all three countries. Service occupations in the U.S. and England, and professional specialty/technical occupations in Canada, are the second most common source of employment for them.

The occupational distributions of women in each country reveal race-immigrant inequality. Both black immigrant and native women are significantly under-represented in high-status white-collar occupations relative to white immigrants and natives. This pattern is evident in all three countries. The index of dissimilarity provides a summary of the unevenness of occupational distributions. White natives are the reference group. In all three countries, of all race-immigrant groups, black immigrants experience the most serious occupational disadvantage relative to white natives, with dissimilarity scores of 12%, 22%, and 31% in Canada, the U.S., and England respectively. The corresponding figures for black natives are 10%, 14%, and 16%, and those for white immigrants are 7%, 11%, and 18%. These patterns indicate that, in each country, black natives have an occupational advantage over black immigrants, a finding supported by statistical comparisons of mean unadjusted occupational status scores within each country. Furthermore, black immigrants have the worst relative outcomes in England, where their dissimilarity score is 31% relative to 12% in Canada and 22% in the U.S. In addition, black immigrants and natives both do less well than white immigrants and natives in the U.S. and Canada. The pattern for England is less straightforward, however, since occupational dissimilarity between white natives and black natives is less than that between white natives and white immigrants. Also, the unadjusted mean occupational status scores of black natives are not significantly different from those of white immigrants and white natives.

Finally, these data patterns reveal that Canadian women experience the least occupational inequality by race-immigrant status, English women the most. Black women, in general, have the best relative outcomes in Canada in terms of occupational dissimilarity scores. Mean scores for black women are also significantly higher in Canada than in the U.S. and England.

Table 6.7 shows that men have distinctly different occupational distributions than women. Overall, men are far more likely than women to be employed in blue-collar as well as executive, administrative, and managerial occupations. They are also significantly less likely to be engaged in service work. Black immigrant men are most highly concentrated in skilled blue-collar and service occupations in the U.S. In Canada and England they are concentrated in skilled and semi-skilled blue-collar occupations. In contrast, black natives are most highly concentrated in unskilled blue-collar and service occupations in the U.S., service and professional specialty/technical occupations in Canada, and skilled blue-collar as well as administrative support occupations in England.

As with women, the occupational patterns reveal race-immigrant inequality. White immigrants and natives are disproportionately represented in executive, managerial, and professional specialty jobs while blacks are mostly concentrated in skilled and unskilled blue-collar ones. In each country, roughly twice as many whites males - immigrant or native - are employed in top occupations as black males. Interestingly, however, in each country, black immigrant men are no more or less likely to be in executive, administrative and managerial positions than black native men. The index of occupational dissimilarity shows that, like their female counterparts, black immigrant men in Canada and England experience the most serious occupational disadvantage of all groups relative to white natives. In Canada, their dissimilarity score is 21% relative to 15% for black natives and 16% for white immigrants. In England, their dissimilarity score is 29% relative to 18% for black natives and 9% for white immigrants. In these two countries, black native men have an occupational advantage over black immigrant men, as supported by differences in mean occupational status scores. In a departure from this pattern, it is black immigrants who have the occupational advantage in the U.S., where 30% of black natives and 23% of black immigrants would have to change occupations in order to achieve distributional parity with white natives.

Canada again seems to have less occupational inequality by race-immigrant status for men while the U.S. and England seem to have similar levels of occupational stratification. In general, blacks have the best occupational outcomes in Canada in terms of dissimilarity scores and mean occupational status scores. Black immigrants have the worst relative outcomes in England (29%) while black natives have the worst in the U.S. (30%). Canada is unique for the unusually high level of occupational dissimilarity between white immigrants and white natives (16%), which slightly surpasses that between black natives and white natives (15%).

Additional indices of occupational dissimilarity (not shown) reveal striking patterns of gender inequality in occupational distribution within race-immigrant group. In order to have the same occupational distribution as men, 39-57% of English women, 24-46% of U.S. women, and 30-43%

of Canadian women would have to change occupations. These patterns indicate greater inequality in the occupational hierarchy of England relative to the U.S. and Canada. Furthermore, the gender difference in each country is largest for black immigrants.

In summary, these results point to a more favorable occupational climate in Canada for blacks than exists in the U.S. and U.K. There is some indication of black native advantage in all three countries for both men and women. The exception is the U.S. where, contrary to theoretical expectations, black immigrant men have an occupational advantage relative to African-Americans. This points to greater inequality between black natives and white natives than between black immigrants and white natives where men are concerned. These results so far support patterns found in recent research (Model, 1997). In general, with rare exceptions, blacks have poorer occupational outcomes relative to whites.

Independent Variables

Tables 6.8 and 6.9 reveal that in the U.S., whites are more likely to be college-educated relative to blacks. This is true for both men and women. Furthermore, there is a black native educational advantage among women at the highest level of educational attainment. African-American women are significantly more likely to get a graduate or professional degree than West Indians. If these women are compared simply on the percent completing a college or postgraduate degree, parity is observed (15% each). African-American men, on the other hand, are less likely than West Indian men to have university qualifications, so black immigrant men have an educational advantage.

Blacks, especially black natives, are significantly more likely to be employed in the public sector relative to whites, who in turn are significantly more likely than blacks to be self-employed. Black natives enjoy greater protection from discrimination in the public sector. White immigrants, on the other hand, seem to use self-employment as an alternate route to upward mobility. This is more true for men than for women. Black immigrants are more likely than other groups to be attending school, and are considerably more likely to be married than black natives. In 1990, 42% and 43% of West Indian women and men, respectively, arrived in the U.S. between 1980 and 1990. In contrast, the patterns for whites reveal a more longstanding migration stream.

In Canada, a significant white-black gap in credentials also exists. For example, among women (Table 6.8), 6% of black immigrants and 21% of white natives or immigrants have a college or postgraduate degree - a difference of 15 percentage points. The difference between black natives and white natives is also large, but is only half that between black immigrants and white natives. These patterns also reveal a substantial black native advantage in education. Black natives - men and women - are roughly twice as likely as black immigrants to have acquired a college or professional degree. This is in stark contrast to the similarity in educational distribution observed for black immigrants and natives in the U.S.

Another key difference between the U.S. and Canada is the relatively lower proportion of whites and black immigrants with college and professional degrees in Canada. For example, among U.S. men (Table 6.9), 14% of black immigrants, 36% of white immigrants, and 33% of white natives have a college or postgraduate degree. In contrast, among Canadian men, 8% of black immigrants, 26% of white immigrants, and 22% of white natives have the same qualifications. While the majority of West Indian migration to the U.S. occurred between 1980 and 1990, West Indian migration to Canada peaked between 1971 and 1981. For example, 46% each of immigrant men and women arrived in Canada between 1971 and 1981 while 42-43% entered the U.S. between 1980 and 1990. As seen in the U.S., the majority of white immigrants have been in Canada for over twenty years. They are also more likely than all other groups to be self-employed and to be married. They are older than other groups and are least likely to be attending school.

British residents are even less likely than Canadians to have college degrees. Again comparing men (Table 6.9), only 15% of white native men have a college or postgraduate degree. The cross-country difference is even starker at the postgraduate level. In England, only 1 and 2% of white native women and men, respectively, have a graduate or professional degree compared with 3 and 5% in Canada, 10 and 13% in the U.S. The latter is far more of a credential society than Canada and

England, with a greater proportion of its population employed in the tertiary (service) sector of the economy (Esping-Andersen, 1993). For emphasis, another comparison shows that in England, 80% and 83% of white native men and women, respectively, have no post-secondary qualifications. This is true for only about 40% each of U.S. and Canadian white native men and women. So, the U.S. population is more well-educated than the Canadian then British populations.

As in Canada and the U.S., gender and race differences in educational attainment are evident in Britain. Among women (Table 6.8), white natives are roughly twice as likely to have a college or postgraduate degree as black natives, and three times as likely as black immigrants. This disparity is even more pronounced for men (Table 6.9) where 15% of white natives have a college or higher degree relative to 3% of black immigrants and 4% of black natives. Only 1% of black immigrant and native men in England have a postgraduate degree. Half as many (.5%) black immigrant and native women have advanced degrees. These patterns suggest that differences in education may function to cement strong race, class, and gender inequality in British society. The cross-country patterns also suggest important differences between the British and North American economies such that the credentialism of the latter - and of the U.S. in particular - is not observed in Britain. That is, in the U.K., a college degree is not a requirement for having a good job or career as is the case in North America. So, cross-national variation in social class or economic structure may provide alternative explanations for cross-country differences observed in the occupational outcomes of West Indians.

Another interesting pattern in England is the youthfulness of the black native population. The average age of black natives in this sample is 26 (for both men and women). This is only ten years younger than the same population in Canada. The average age of other immigrant groups in each country range from 35 to 48. It is possible that the youth of the black native populations in England and Canada is indicative of their status as predominantly second generation West Indians - whose parents migrated during the 1950s and 1960s.

As observed in the U.S. and Canada, West Indian immigrants are more likely to be self-employed than black natives. Whites are more likely to be self-employed than blacks, in general, and white immigrants are roughly three times more likely than black immigrants to use self-employment as an alternate route to upward mobility. West Indian immigrants to Britain are much older than any other immigrant group. They are also far more likely to be married than other groups and are less likely to attend school than black natives.

Overall, interesting similarities exist across all three countries, such as strong black-white differences in educational attainment, marriage prevalence, and self-employment. Among women in each country, black natives tend to have either educational advantage or educational parity relative to black immigrants. This is true for black men in Canada and England. In contrast, among black men in the U.S., there is immigrant-native parity for completion· of bachelor's degrees and immigrant advantage in postgraduate education. These patterns of black immigrant-native educational differences are similar to those observed for occupational differences. Black men in the U.S. are distinct in their departure from the typical pattern observed for women in the U.S. and for black men and women in other countries.

In addition, there are noticeable cross-country differences in educational attainment for men and women. The largest differences in educational attainment between white natives and black natives or between white natives and black immigrants exist in the U.S. This is despite the fact that black immigrants and natives - male and female - are significantly more likely to have university qualifications in the U.S. relative to Canada and England (with one exception: black natives are no more likely to have higher education in the U.S. than in Canada). In general, levels of education are higher in the U.S. than in Canada than in England, suggesting that closer examination of differences in social stratification systems (economic and educational structures) may be needed.

Table 6.1: Country-Specific Labor Force Participation Rates by Race, Immigrant Status and Gender

Race and Immigrant Status	United States, 1990		Canada, 1991		England, 1991	
	Men	Women	Men	Women	Men	Women
White natives	87.4	70.8	88.8	75.4	85.6	65.6
White immigrants	86.1	61.6	90.7	74.2	79.7	62.3
Black natives	74.6	67.6	73.3	72.4	84.7	68.2
Black immigrants	84.5	79.4	87.6	80.0	83.3	68.4

Table 6.2: Country-Specific Logistic Regression Analysis of Labor Force Participation

Variables	U.S., 1990	Canada, 1991	England, 1991
Age	0.266***	0.304***	0.167***
Age squared	-0.003***	-0.004***	-0.003***
Gender (1=Male)	0.199***	0.067	1.247***
Black native	-0.262***	-0.178*	0.013
Foreign-born white [a]	----	----	-0.231**
Foreign-born black [a]	----	----	0.529***
FB white, duration 0-10 yrs.	-0.868***	-0.343*	----
FB white, duration >10 yrs.	-0.241***	0.009	----
FB black, duration 0-10 yrs.	0.019	-0.222*	----
FB black, duration >10 yrs.	0.441***	0.081	----
(Reference: white native)	----	----	----
Own child < 6 yrs. only [b]	-0.596***	-1.060***	-1.369***
Enrollment in school	-0.751***	-0.620***	-5.201***
Work-limiting Disability [c]	-2.249***	----	-2.625***

Table 6.2 *continued*

Variables	U.S., 1990	Canada, 1991	England, 1991
Post high-school education	0.679***	0.780***	0.823***
Married [d]	-0.674**	-0.402***	-0.136+
Married*Gender	1.563***	1.581***	0.770***
Intercept	-3.064***	-3.368***	-0.122
-2 Log L	33889.4	2193.8	7651.7
(df)	(14)	(13)	(12)
N	39,107	11,817	10,729

* p<.05; ** p<.01; *** p<.001; + p<.10

[a] Foreign-born-status variables (race-specific) are typically cross-tabulated with duration of time in receiving country except where no duration data are available. The models including foreign-born status*duration crosstabs are "best models" compared with those omitting duration. The U.K. Census data lack duration information.

[b] In the U.S., this variable means: presence in the household of own children less than 6 years old only. In Canada, this variable means: presence in the Census family (which can be a subset of the household unit) of own children less than 6 years old only. In both countries, this information is coded only for women aged 15 and over. In the U.K., this variable means: presence in the household unit of dependent children and it is coded for both men and women. No information is available about the age of dependent children.

[c] No information about disability is available in the Canadian census.

[d] In England, the "married" category may contain separated people. No distinction is made between "married, living together" and "married, separated."

Table 6.3: Gender-specific Logistic Regression Analysis of Labor Force Participation, U.S. 1990

Variables	MEN	WOMEN
Age	0.310***	0.238***
Age squared	-0.004***	-0.003***
Race*Immigrant Status*Duration: (ref: native white)		
Black native	-0.631***	-0.072
FB white in the U.S. 1-10 yrs.	-0.911***	-0.884***
FB white in the U.S. >10 yrs.	-0.142+	-0.266***
Car.-born black in the U.S. 1-10 yrs.	-0.522***	0.303***
Car.-born black in the U.S. >10 yrs.	0.023	0.636***
Own child under 6 yrs. in household	N/A	-0.547***
Enrollment in school	-1.126***	-0.529***
Work-limiting Disability	-2.663***	-1.888***
Post high-school education	0.471***	0.767***
Married	0.856***	-0.543***
Intercept	-2.964***	-2.944***
N	18,087	21,020
-2 Log L (df)	11731.42 (11)	21836.61 (12)

* $p<.05$; ** $p<.01$; *** $p<.001$; + $p<.10$

Table 6.4: Gender-specific Logistic Regression Analysis of Labor Force Participation, Canada 1991

Variables	MEN	WOMEN
Age	0.334***	0.282***
Age squared	-0.005***	-0.004***
Race*Immigrant Status*Duration: (ref: native white)		
Canada-born Caribbean black	-0.401**	-0.025
FB white in Canada 1-10 yrs.	-0.093	-0.393*
FB white in Canada >10 yrs.	-0.042	0.046
Car.-born black in Canada 1-10 yrs.	-0.696***	0.020
Car.-born black in Canada >10 yrs.	-0.074	0.175+
Own child under 6 yrs. in household	N/A	-1.018***
Enrollment in school	-0.886***	-0.465***
Post high-school education	0.737***	0.780***
Married	1.091***	-0.294***
Intercept	-3.412***	-3.223***
N	5,516	6,301
-2 Log L (df)	1091.68 (10)	910.16 (11)

* p<.05; ** p<.01; *** p≤.001; + p<.10

Table 6.5: Gender-specific Logistic Regression Analysis of Labor Force Participation, U.K. 1991

Variables	MEN	WOMEN
Age	0.186***	0.168***
Age squared	-0.003***	-0.003***
Race*Immigrant Status: (ref: native white)		
England-born Caribbean black	-0.224	0.157
Caribbean-born black	-0.031	0.709***
White foreign born	-0.493**	-0.157
Dependent child	-0.116	-1.759***
Enrollment in school	-6.346***	-4.123***
Work-limiting Disability	-3.337***	-2.096***
Post high-school education	0.262	0.994***
Married	0.472***	-0.543***
Intercept	1.031	-0.109
N	5,043	5,686
-2 Log L (df)	2120.286 (10)	5262.309 (10)

* $p<.05$; ** $p<.01$; *** $p<.001$; + $p<.10$

.

Table 6.6: Cross-national Occupational Statistics for Women

Occupation (percent in)	US (1990)				Canada (1991)				England (1991)			
	Black FB	Black native	White FB	White native	Black FB	Black native	White FB	White native	Black FB	Black native	White FB	White native
Executive, Administrative and Managerial	7.9	10.1	13.0	14.0	8.4	8.8	16.8	12.2	4.4	8.1	12.7	11.0
Professional Specialty, Technical & Related support	18.0	16.2	21.3	22.8	23.3	19.3	25.6	24.2	21.0	13.8	23.4	16.4
Sales	9.2	10.7	14.9	14.0	7.0	13.4	10.3	10.0	2.1	7.9	5.4	10.8
Administrative support, including Clerical	26.5	31.2	25.2	31.0	31.9	35.7	31.4	35.1	21.2	46.2	22.4	32.8
Service (all)	32.8	21.8	15.0	11.4	15.6	16.0	9.8	10.9	38.2	17.1	28.8	21.9
Farming, Forestry and Fishing	0.2	0.3	0.2	0.5	0.3	0.7	0.1	0.6	0	0	0.1	0
Precision Production, Craft and Repair	1.1	1.6	3.7	1.6	2.4	1.5	1.1	1.0	3.6	2.8	3.4	1.7
Machine Operators, Assemblers and Inspectors	3.1	5.1	5.5	2.6	6.3	0.7	1.7	1.6	9.1	3.7	3.8	4.7
Transport. and Material Moving	1.2	3.1	1.3	2.2	0.4	0.6	0.9	1.1	0.4	0.4	0.1	0.7
Miscellaneous (Canada only)	--	--	--	--	4.5	3.2	2.4	3.4	--	--	--	--

Table 6.6 *continued*

	US (1990)				Canada (1991)				England (1991)			
	Black FB	Black native	White FB	White native	Black FB	Black native	White FB	White native	Black FB	Black native	White FB	White native
INDEX OF DISSIMILARITY	**22.3**	**14.3**	**10.5**	**(Ref.)**	**11.9**	**9.8**	**6.5**	**(Ref.)**	**30.9**	**15.6**	**17.7**	**(Ref.)**
Mean ISEI Score (Standard deviation)	42.2 (15.6)	45.2 (15.3)	48.9 (15.4)	50.5 (14.1)	45.9 (10.8)	48.0 (11.3)	50.6 (11.0)	49.6 (11.3)	37.2 (13.0)	43.4 (11.9)	43.7 (15.9)	44.1 (14.1)
Number of cases	4962	4567	3387	4441	1663	680	1451	1375	1031	1057	1003	1129

79

Table 6.7: Cross-national Occupational Statistics for Men

Occupation (percent in)	US (1990)				Canada (1991)				England (1991)			
	Black FB	Black native	White FB	White native	Black FB	Black native	White FB	White native	Black FB	Black native	White FB	White native
Executive, Administrative and Managerial	8.7	8.0	17.7	18.1	9.2	10.6	24.5	17.8	6.7	7.7	17.6	15.9
Professional Specialty, Technical & Related support	10.8	10.5	21.8	19.4	10.9	15.5	23.8	16.4	6.7	12.0	18.1	17.8
Sales	7.2	6.9	13.1	12.6	6.3	12.8	8.7	11.0	1.5	8.9	3.4	3.8
Administrative support, including Clerical	12.6	12.4	5.0	7.2	13.7	14.0	7.0	9.3	6.7	17.8	8.1	12.2
Service (all)	17.1	19.8	9.6	9.3	11.3	17.0	6.4	10.5	12.6	11.6	13.4	8.8
Farming, Forestry and Fishing	1.4	1.9	1.1	1.9	0.5	1.4	1.3	2.5	0	0.1	0.3	0.4
Precision Production, Craft and Repair	21.1	12.3	19.3	17.5	12.6	6.6	8.8	9.9	32.7	26.8	24.6	24.3
Machine Operators, Assemblers and Inspectors	7.8	7.9	4.5	5.1	20.7	6.6	11.0	9.1	18.7	9.0	7.9	8.5
Transport. and Material Moving	13.3	20.3	7.9	9.0	6.3	5.8	3.5	6.1	14.1	6.0	6.6	8.2
Miscellaneous (Canada only)	--	--	--	--	8.5	9.6	5.1	7.5	--	--	--	--

Table 6.7 *continued*

	US (1990)				Canada (1991)				England (1991)			
	Black FB	Black native	White FB	White native	Black FB	Black native	White FB	White native	Black FB	Black native	White FB	White native
INDEX OF DISSIMILARITY	23.9	30.0	7.8	(Ref.)	20.8	15.2	16.0	(Ref.)	29.1	17.8	9.0	(Ref.)
Mean ISEI Score	40.1	39.2	48.4	47.8	41.0	43.9	48.3	45.1	35.2	39.4	42.8	43.2
(Standard deviation)	(15.2)	(15.3)	(17.7)	(17.5)	(12.3)	(13.0)	(13.8)	(13.7)	(11.2)	(11.8)	(16.0)	(14.9)
Number of cases	4014	3777	4042	4656	1326	634	1583	1501	931	844	1021	1253

81

Table 6.8: Sample Means and Standard Deviations (in parentheses) for Independent Variables: Women

Variables	U.S., 1990				Canada, 1991				England, 1991			
	Black FB	Black native	White FB	White native	Black FB	Black native	White FB	White native	Black FB	Black native	White FB	White native
Age	37.9 (12.0)	36.1 (12.5)	42.1 (12.6)	37.6 (12.9)	38.0 (11.3)	28.1 (10.8)	41.5 (12.0)	35.6 (12.1)	45.8 (10.6)	26.6 (6.4)	39.0 (13.2)	36.6 (13.2)
Educational Qualification: [a]												
No post-secondary	.55	.51	.45	.40	.40	.42	.35	.39	.85	.89	.75	.83
Post-sec., no univ. degree	.31	.34	.29	.33	.54	.45	.43	.40	.13	.05	.10	.07
B.A. or equivalent	.11	.10	.15	.18	.05	.11	.15	.18	.02	.05	.13	.09
Post B.A. degree	.04	.05	.11	.10	.01	.02	.06	.03	.01	.004	.03	.01
Immigrant duration (yrs.)												
- 0-10	.42		.23		.31		.12		nav		nav	
- 11-20	.37	—	.24	—	.46	nav	.28	—		—		—
>20	.21		.54		.23		.61					

82

Table 6.8 *continued*

Variables	U.S., 1990					Canada, 1991				England, 1991		
	Black FB	Black native	White FB	White native	Black FB	Black native	White FB	White native	Black FB	Black native	White FB	White native
Class of worker (US only):												
Private	.79	.69	.77	.78	—							
Public	.17	.29	.12	.15								
Self-employment	.04	.03	.12	.07								
Self-employment=1; 0=Otherwise (UK & Can.)	—	—	—	—	.01 (.12)	.01 (.11)	.05 (.21)	.03 (.17)	.02 (.13)	.01 (.11)	.06 (.24)	.03 (.18)
School attendance=1; 0=Otherwise	.20 (.40)	.18 (.38)	.12 (.32)	.16 (.37)	.23 (.42)	.45 (.50)	.18 (.38)	.23 (.42)	.01 (.09)	.05 (.21)	.04 (.19)	.04 (.19)
Married=1; 0=Otherwise	.44 (.50)	.33 (.47)	.66 (.47)	.56 (.50)	.46 (.50)	.30 (.46)	.68 (.46)	.58 (.49)	.46 (.50)	.15 (.35)	.49 (.50)	.43 (.50)
Number of cases	4962	4567	3387	4441	1663	680	1451	1375	1031	1057	1003	1129

[a] See table 5.2 for definition of this variable.

83

Table 6.9: Sample Means and Standard Deviations (in parentheses) for Independent Variables: Men

Variables	U.S., 1990				Canada, 1991				England, 1991			
	Black FB	Black native	White FB	White native	Black FB	Black native	White FB	White native	Black FB	Black native	White FB	White native
Age	37.8 (12.1)	36.7 (13.0)	42.2 (12.5)	38.2 (13.1)	37.9 (12.0)	27.8 (11.0)	42.1 (12.2)	35.1 (12.2)	48.2 (10.7)	26.3 (6.6)	41.2 (13.0)	38.6 (13.5)
Educational Qualification: [a]												
No post-secondary	.60	.60	.42	.39	.45	.47	.27	.40	.95	.92	.80	.80
Post-sec., no univ. degree	.26	.27	.22	.28	.47	.38	.47	.38	.02	.04	.04	.05
B.A. or equivalent	.09	.08	.18	.20	.06	.13	.17	.17	.02	.03	.12	.13
Post B.A. degree	.05	.04	.18	.13	.02	.02	.09	.05	.01	.01	.04	.02
Immigrant duration (yrs.)												
- 0-10	.43	—	.28	—	.31	—	.11	—	nav	—	nav	—
- 11-20	.36		.26		.46		.28					
>20	.20		.46		.23		.62					

Table 6.9 *continued*

Variables	U.S., 1990				Canada, 1991				England, 1991			
	Black FB	Black native	White FB	White native	Black FB	Black native	White FB	White native	Black FB	Black native	White FB	White native
Class of worker (US only):												
Private	.79	.73	.71	.74								
Public	.15	.22	.08	.13								
Self-employment	.07	.05	.21	.13								
Self-employment=1; 0=Otherwise (UK & Can.)	—	—	—	—	.04 (.19)	.04 (.19)	.07 (.25)	.06 (.24)	.07 (.26)	.05 (.22)	.15 (.36)	.13 (.33)
School attendance=1; 0=Otherwise	.17 (.38)	.14 (.35)	.11 (.31)	.13 (.34)	.17 (.37)	.44 (.50)	.12 (.32)	.20 (.40)	.01 (.09)	.03 (.18)	.04 (.19)	.03 (.16)
Married=1; 0=Otherwise	.57 (.50)	.43 (.50)	.72 (.45)	.60 (.49)	.65 (.48)	.30 (.46)	.73 (.44)	.56 (.50)	.59 (.49)	.13 (.34)	.51 (.50)	.48 (.50)
Number of cases	4014	3777	4042	4656	1326	634	1583	1501	931	844	1021	1253

[a] See table 5.2 for definition of this variable.

CHAPTER 7
Occupational Attainment in the U.S., Canada and England

Recent studies have shown that U.S.-born West Indian males, as well as foreign-born West Indian males who have lived in the U.S. for at least twelve years, have better net earnings and occupational outcomes than African-American males (Model 1997; Kalmijn, 1996; Dodoo, 1997). Foreign-born West Indian women also show a net earnings - but not occupational - advantage relative to African-American women (Model 1997). U.S.-born West Indian women, on the other hand, have both an earnings and occupational advantage. Attempts to explain these ethnic differences in socioeconomic outcomes have led researchers to comparative research. To what extent do arguments of West Indian cultural superiority, immigrant selectivity, or employer favoritism hold true when U.S. results are compared with those from England and Canada, two other major receiving countries for Caribbean immigrants? Canada and England do not have an established native black population, so that immigrant-native comparisons, which typically tap ethnic differences in the U.S., tend to be really first versus second-or-higher generation comparisons in Canada and England. However, national comparisons have helped to further debunk arguments of West Indian cultural superiority. Caribbean immigrants do not have the same outstanding socioeconomic outcomes in the U.K. and Canada as they do in the U.S. relative to black natives (Freeman, 1987; Segal, 1987; Model and Ladipo, 1996; Model, 1997).

The race versus ethnicity debate is an intriguing one. If West Indians have better socioeconomic outcomes than African-Americans, to what extent can the poorer outcomes of African-Americans relative to whites be due to racial discrimination? However, there is still one overarching issue of concern to this study: regardless of West Indian socioeconomic advantage in the U.S., race still functions to limit the outcomes of BOTH West Indians and African-Americans relative to whites. For both ethnic groups, there is a social cost of being black. Blacks - immigrant or native - also do less well than whites in England and Canada (Karn, 1997; King, 1995).

This study examines the extent to which education counteracts the negative effects of a confluence of different disadvantaged statuses, namely race, immigrant status and gender, in the United States, Canada and England. National comparisons are important because Caribbean adaptation - like Caribbean migration - occurs in a global context. How may national socio-political factors inform observed cross-national differences or similarities in the occupational outcomes of black immigrants? Will education have the same mitigating effect in each country?

MULTIVARIATE RESULTS[12]

The following multivariate analyses examine national differences in the occupational attainment of black and white immigrants and natives. Occupational attainment is measured by the International Socioeconomic Index of Occupations (ISEI). In each country, the reference group for blacks and white immigrants is white natives. Preliminary OLS analyses run on the total sample in each country (see Appendix) confirm that being black and being immigrant negatively and significantly impact occupational status. Interestingly, gender (coded 1 for men) has a negative effect on ISEI. Since this effect is in the opposite direction from the expected, subsequent analyses are done separately by gender to explore differences in the occupational experiences of men and women.

In the main analyses, OLS regressions for men and women were done separately by country. Model 1 examines the effect of race-immigrant status on occupational attainment, controlling for age. Model 2 examines the race-immigrant effect controlling for age and educational differences between groups. Model 3 is a full immigrant attainment model with controls for a) compositional differences among groups that are relevant to occupational outcomes and b) local contextual factors that may confound the effects of individual-level variables. Model 4 explores interaction effects between education and duration-specific race-immigrant status. In order to test for additional interaction effects, t-tests were done to check for significant difference in regression coefficients 1) within country between men and women and 2) across country by race-immigrant status. Tests were also done for the effect of race-immigrant status on occupational attainment within models (that is, between categories of race-immigrant dummies). This allows a more precise determination of whether race-immigrant groups differ significantly amongst themselves and not only in relation to white natives.

While descriptive analyses provide support for segmented assimilation theories - by revealing diversity of human capital and occupational characteristics, entrepreneurship, and occupational niching among immigrants - I expect that multivariate analyses will reveal some neo-Marxist patterns of race-immigrant differences in socioeconomic outcomes. For example, I expect that women will be disadvantaged relative to men and that black immigrant women will have poorer outcomes relative to black immigrant men (and indirectly relative to white native men). I also expect that immigrant duration and education will have positive effects on immigrant status in support of neo-classical assimilation theory. Furthermore, I expect to find interactive effects of education and race-immigrant status (duration-specific in Canada and the U.S.) for men and women. In addition, I expect that England, with the least facilitating socio-political context, will have poorer outcomes for native and immigrant blacks. Education should be less effective in mitigating race or immigrant status in England relative to Canada and the U.S. I expect that blacks - native or immigrant - in the U.S. will have better net occupational outcomes than those in Canada partly because of a U.S. socio-political context that includes stronger anti-discrimination protection for minorities. However, because of Canada's multicultural socio-political context, immigrant and native minority outcomes should be similar to those in the U.S. so that North American outcomes will be distinct from English ones.

The United States

Model 1, Table 7.1 reveals that while both black and native women are disadvantaged in occupational attainment relative to white natives, the black foreign-born are particularly disadvantaged. Immigrant status has a negative effect on occupational outcomes so that both white and black immigrants have poorer outcomes relative to white natives. However, race also has a negative impact so that black natives are disadvantaged relative to white natives. Furthermore, black immigrants have a "double disadvantage" as evidenced by a much larger occupational deficit than black natives. The relative positioning of these groups supports neo-Marxist theories. Model 2 shows that education has a positive effect on occupational outcomes, with gains to occupational status as educational qualifications increase. The strong negative effects of race-immigrant status are reduced once compositional differences in educational attainment are controlled. However, race still has a strong negative impact, especially for the foreign-born. Thus, both neoclassical assimilation and neo-Marxist theories are supported.

Model 3 reveals an assimilation effect for black and white immigrants. Those with longer duration of time in the U.S. are less disadvantaged relative to white natives. In fact, white immigrants who have lived in the U.S. for twenty or more years are at occupational parity, net of other factors. Race continues to have a particularly negative effect since for black immigrants duration is not quite as positive. In fact, for these immigrants, a duration period of over twenty years is no more beneficial to occupational attainment than one of eleven to twenty years. So, immigrant status has a more negative effect for blacks than for whites, and duration is more beneficial for white than for black immigrants.

Does education mitigate the effect of race-immigrant status? The interaction model in Table 7.1 (model 4), shows that the answer is yes. Adjusted means calculated from regression outcomes reveal, for example, that black natives with a postgraduate degree come closest to achieving parity of occupational status with white natives (Table 7.7).[13]   The adjusted mean for white native women with a graduate or professional degree is 63. That for black native women is 62. The (significant) interaction coefficients for this group reveal incremental progress towards parity of occupational status as qualifications increase.

Black immigrants, with a "double disadvantage," do not realize the same gains as black natives. For them, education tempers the effect of race-immigrant status but not enough to allow them to attain near-parity with white natives at any level of educational attainment. Table 7.1, model 4 reveals that duration continues to lessen the negative effects of immigrant status in a pattern consistent with assimilation. At the same time, education counteracts the negative effect of race-immigrant status, operating to allow additional closing of the occupational gap between black immigrants and white natives. However, at all duration levels, education fails to mitigate race-immigrant status for the most highly qualified immigrants. Among immigrants who have been in the U.S. twenty or fewer years, those with advanced degrees have the same or slightly lower adjusted mean occupational status scores as black immigrants with a B.A.   This puts them at even greater relative disadvantage than immigrants of other qualifications. If these degrees are earned outside of the U.S., the results support previous findings of a devaluation of foreign credentials. However, for those immigrants who earned their degrees in the U.S., the results imply that, in competition with black natives for higher status white-collar jobs, regardless of time spent in the U.S. labor market, immigrants are at a disadvantage because a) they are never able to gain access to some of the same high-quality networks or other job-related resources as natives or b) employers prefer to hire black natives for higher-status jobs.

For white immigrants, education also has a mitigating effect on race-immigrant status. However, this interactive effect plays out differently for white immigrants than it does for black immigrants. White immigrants are initially less disadvantaged relative to white natives than are black immigrants.   Duration also functions in model 4 to decrease white immigrant disadvantage over time, bringing them far closer than black immigrants to parity with white natives. For white immigrants who have been in the U.S. for twenty or fewer years, education has no significant mitigating effect on immigrant disadvantage, in general. At a duration of over twenty years, education counteracts the negative effect of immigrant status so that white immigrants actually have higher mean occupational status scores than similarly qualified white natives. Thus, white immigrants who have lived in the U.S. for over twenty years benefit not only from the direct effects of duration and educational qualification, but also from the mitigating effect of education on race-immigrant status, which boosts the status scores of college-educated to above-parity levels over time. This contrasts with model 3 in which, net of education and other factors, the assimilative effect of duration results in parity for white immigrants of longest duration.

How similar are the experiences of men? Table 7.2, model 1 reveals significant negative effects of race. Both black natives and black immigrants have lower occupational status than white natives. Unlike the pattern for women, in this preliminary model, black immigrants suffer no double disadvantage. They do no worse than black natives. In fact, in model 2, once educational differences are controlled, black immigrants have slightly better outcomes than black natives. The smaller race-immigrant effects for blacks in this model suggest that much of the occupational gap between blacks and whites is a function of educational differences. Also in contrast with the pattern for women, white foreign-born men are not distinctly different from white natives, so they suffer no immigrant disadvantage. Thus, contrary to assimilation or neo-Marxist theories, the foreign-born do no worse than natives, and black immigrants suffer no double disadvantage. There is, however, a clear disadvantage of race.

Model 3 elaborates on model 2 to show that, net of other factors, duration has limited effects on occupational attainment for male immigrants. Black immigrants who have been in the U.S. for ten or fewer years do less well than those who have been in the U.S. for eleven or more years. There is no significant difference between a duration of eleven to twenty years and that of twenty or more years. Again, black natives do not differ significantly from black immigrants at any duration of time in the U.S. All together, these patterns provide very weak support for double disadvantage, and only where recent black immigrants are concerned. White immigrants do suffer a disadvantage relative to white natives during their first twenty years in the U.S. A duration period of ten or fewer years is not significantly different from one of eleven to twenty years. However, after twenty years in the U.S., the white foreign-born experience occupational parity with white natives, in support of assimilation theory.

Interestingly, while education mitigates race-immigrant status for black women, it provides no mitigating effect for black men, immigrant or native (model 4). In fact, black immigrant men with a duration of over twenty years and a bachelor's degree have an even greater disadvantage relative to white natives than black natives and other black immigrants. Mean adjusted occupational status scores illustrate this. Comparing men with a bachelor's degree (Table 7.7), the mean score is 57 for white natives, 54 for black natives and recent black immigrants, 54 for black immigrants with a duration of eleven to twenty years, and 51 for black immigrants with a duration of over twenty years. Rather than mitigating the effect of race-immigrant status, education may be an additional source of disadvantage for immigrants who have been in the U.S. for a very long time and have a college degree. Overall, however, there is parity of occupational status between black natives and black immigrants who have lived in the U.S. for twenty or fewer years, as well as immigrant advantage at higher levels of duration. Of note, both black groups are significantly less successful than whites in general.

Education also has mixed interactive effects for white immigrants. Those who have lived in the U.S. for ten or fewer years actually suffer intensified disadvantage with higher levels of education (Table 7.2, model 4). This results in a pattern of initial immigrant occupational advantage (that is, within the first ten years of entry into the U.S.) for those *without* a college or higher degree and initial occupational disadvantage for those with a bachelor's or postgraduate degree. Given the duration at which this interactive effect is observed, these results provide stronger support for the argument of immigrant disadvantage due to the devaluation of foreign credentials than do the results for black immigrants. For emphasis, model 4 clarifies that the negative effect of immigrant status revealed in model 3 for whites during their first ten years in the U.S. is really limited to those with a college or postgraduate degree. White immigrants without a degree have higher occupational attainment initially than similarly qualified white natives, which does not support assimilation theory. In addition, immigrants who have lived in the U.S. for at least eleven years have parity of occupational attainment with white natives. The exceptions are a) white immigrants at a duration of eleven to twenty years for whom a graduate or professional degree is devalued, resulting in immigrant disadvantage and b) white immigrants at a duration of over twenty years for whom a post-secondary education results in occupational advantage relative to white natives.

The pattern of results reveal key differences in the occupational experiences of men and women. For example, while there is a double disadvantage for women of being black and immigrant, race is the primary source of disadvantage for men. Women also receive significantly fewer returns to their educational investment than men. For example, a postgraduate degree increases occupational status scores by 17 points for women, while men are rewarded an increase of 29 points for the same degree (model 4, Tables 7.1 and 7.2). Furthermore, the relative effects of immigrant status are significantly worse for black women than for black men, in support of neo-Marxist theoretical expectations of triple disadvantage. However, the interactive effects of education with race-immigrant status allow some black women to gain additional returns to education. In general, education is better at mitigating the negative effects of race-immigrant status for women than for men.[14]

In summary, there is mixed support for assimilation and neo-Marxist theories. Human capital and duration of time in the U.S. have positive effects on occupational attainment. However, results vary by gender, race, and immigrant status. Unlike most men in this sample, female immigrants suffer an initial occupational disadvantage which declines with time in the U.S. In support of neo-Marxist conflict expectations, there is a double disadvantage of race and immigrant status. Furthermore, women have lower returns to education than men. In addition, black women suffer a greater loss of occupational status due to race-immigrant status than do black men, which supports the neo-Marxist triple disadvantage hypothesis. On the other hand, education functions to mitigate some of the negative effects of race for black natives, immigrant status for whites, and double disadvantage for black immigrants. The results for men provide very weak support for traditional patterns of assimilation. Among black men, there is no immigrant disadvantage per se, so that black natives and black immigrants are equally disadvantaged relative to white natives. Unlike the case for women, education rarely mitigates disadvantage for black men. Among white men, with a few exceptions, immigrant status denotes either parity with or advantage over white natives. However, advanced degrees for recent white immigrant males are significantly devalued.

Canada

Table 7.3, model 1 reveals that, surprisingly, black native women are not significantly disadvantaged occupationally relative to white natives. This does not support neo-Marxist conflict theory. On the other hand, there is evidence in suggestion of double disadvantage for black immigrant women. These women have significantly worse relative outcomes than black natives. While this may initially suggest that there is no disadvantage of race per se but rather of immigrant status, a comparison of black immigrants with white immigrants reveals otherwise. Immigrant status for white women is positive, that for blacks is negative. Had immigrant status been the only handicap for black women, one would expect the experiences of both sets of immigrants to be similar. However, they are significantly different. Controlling for educational differences among groups (model 2), neither white immigrants nor black natives have significantly different occupational outcomes relative to white natives. Black immigrants, however, continue to be the most disadvantaged of all groups, in support of neo-Marxist conflict theory. Do these findings persist when other relevant variables are controlled?

Net of other individual-level and contextual factors (model 3), black natives continue to have occupational parity with white natives. The results for immigrants are qualified by duration of time in the Canadian labor market. In this, the model of best fit, both black and white immigrants benefit from increased time in the Canadian labor market in support of assimilation theory. As in the U.S., however, duration results in different outcomes for black and white immigrants. Duration shrinks the gap in occupational status between black immigrants and white natives so that adjusted mean occupational scores for immigrants who have lived in Canada for over twenty years come very close to parity with white natives. However, at no time do black immigrants actually achieve occupational parity with white natives, which is also the case in the U.S. overall. Interestingly, Caribbean immigrants with a duration of twenty or more years have adjusted mean occupational status scores that are not significantly different from the scores of black natives, who are second-generation Caribbean immigrants in the Canadian context. As mentioned before, the experiences of white immigrants are different from those of black immigrants. Initially disadvantaged relative to white natives, white immigrants attain occupational parity after living in Canada for eleven to twenty years. Furthermore, those who have lived in Canada for over twenty years actually have a net occupational advantage relative to white natives.

In contrast with the U.S., education does not mitigate the effects of immigrant status or race for women in Canada. The interactive model (4, Table 7.3) does not provide a significantly better fit to the data than the additive model (3, Table 7.3). There is some suggestion, however, that net of other factors, black natives with a bachelor's degree are significantly disadvantaged relative to white natives with the same degree. The former apparently rank lower than white natives in employers' labor queues where white-collar jobs are concerned. Black immigrants with twenty or fewer years of experience in the Canadian labor market receive an additional benefit from having some post-secondary qualifications. In addition, there is some suggestion that education mitigates race-immigrant status for black immigrants with a duration of eleven or more years by significantly boosting the occupational status of those with a postgraduate or professional degree. The boost would actually allow this particular group of black immigrants to have higher occupational status than white (and black) natives with the same level of qualifications. These interactive results, however, are tentative. No mitigating effects of education are observed for white immigrants.

Thus far, results for Canadian women are very similar to those of American women although the paths to these outcomes vary. Overall, education and duration have positive effects on occupational attainment in support of assimilation theory. There is also an initial disadvantage of immigrant status that declines with time in receiving country. However, the experiences of immigrants vary by race. Black immigrants never attain parity with white natives, according to the model of best fit in each country. Rather, in each country, double disadvantage is observed in support of neo-Marxist conflict theory. In other words, black native women have a consistent occupational advantage over black immigrant women in both countries, on average. On the other hand, white immigrants' initial occupational disadvantage disappears with time in receiving country so that after spending more than twenty years in North American economies, white immigrants actually have an occupational advantage relative to white natives. In the U.S., this advantage is the result of the mitigating effect of education on race-immigrant status while in Canada this "bonus" effect of education is not necessary. Likewise, in the U.S., black natives (mostly African-American) achieve near-parity with whites because of the mitigating effect of educational qualifications while in Canada, parity for black natives (second-generation Caribbean) is observed in simpler models.

How do the experiences of men compare with those for women? The occupational outcomes of black native men are not significantly different from those of white native men (Table 7.4, model 1). This is true across all models. So as with women, there is no support for a neo-Marxist conflict hypothesis of racial disadvantage for natives. On the other hand, there is support of the conflict hypothesis of double disadvantage. Immigrant status is far more negative for Caribbean immigrants than for white immigrants, and this holds true even in models with individual- and contextual-level controls. As observed with women, white immigrants have a persistent occupational advantage relative to white natives.

In clear contrast to the pattern for American and Canadian women, and in consistency with the pattern for American men, Table 7.4, model 3 shows that duration has limited effects on occupational outcomes for men. While black immigrants with a duration of fewer than ten years in Canada seem to have more of an occupational disadvantage relative to immigrants of longer duration, there really is no significant benefit of duration for this group of men. Twenty years of experience in the Canadian (or American) labor market is no more beneficial than less than ten years of experience for black immigrant men. As with Canadian women, there is some suggestion in model 4 that education mitigates the effect of race-immigrant status to allow black immigrants with a postgraduate or professional degree to surpass white (and black) natives with the same qualifications. This occurs at a duration of less than ten or greater than twenty years in Canada. However, these results are tentative since model 3 is the model of best fit. Thus, overall, education does not have a mitigating effect on race-immigrant status for black men, in consistency with U.S. results. Of note, while the results for the U.S. indicate that race, rather than race and immigrant status, is the key source of disadvantage for men, in Canada there is double disadvantage since outcomes for black immigrants are worse than those for white immigrants and black natives. More explicitly, in the U.S., black immigrant and native men are "in the same boat." In Canada, however, black natives (the Caribbean second-generation) have a clear occupational advantage relative to Caribbean immigrants.

The patterns for white immigrant men reveal occupational parity with white natives at a duration of twenty years or less, and immigrant advantage at a duration of twenty or more years (as confirmed by statistical tests).[15] Unlike the case with the U.S., the qualifications of white immigrants - who tend to be more highly educated than white natives in the Canadian context - are not devalued initially. Overall, results for white male immigrants to North America reveal that traditional patterns of assimilation are not completely supported. There is no initial immigrant disadvantage upon entry into the receiving economy, with the exception of college-educated white immigrants to the U.S., for whom qualifications are devalued. In general, immigrants with eleven to twenty years of experience in the North American economies experience parity with white natives. Those with a duration of twenty or more years experience occupational parity in the U.S. and immigrant advantage in Canada. White immigrants consistently have better occupational outcomes than black immigrants, net of relevant factors.

So far, the occupational experiences of Canadian men and women have been described, with frequent mention of where experiences are similar or different. There are a few other key differences worth mentioning. While the returns to education are lower in Canada than in the U.S. overall, rewards to education are significantly lower for college-educated women than for similarly qualified men. Canadian men with a bachelor's degree are rewarded with an increase of 15 occupational status scores while similarly qualified women are rewarded with an increase of 12 (relative to those without qualifications). A postgraduate degree is rewarded with an increase of 20 points for men and 18 for women. Interestingly, the gender difference in rewards to educational investment is not as large as in the U.S. In addition, the effects of race-immigrant status are not significantly worse for women than for men, on average. However, white women with a duration of fewer than ten years in Canada tend to do less well initially than white male immigrants with the same duration (that is, in comparison with their native counterparts). Also, among blacks, immigrant women with a duration of twenty or more years in Canada tend to have poorer relative outcomes than black men of the same duration. This provides very weak support for the conflict hypothesis of triple disadvantage.

England

The pattern of results for black women in England are initially similar to those for black women in the U.S. Table 7.5, model 1 shows that black natives (also second-generation Caribbean in this context) are occupationally disadvantaged relative to white natives. Furthermore, race-immigrant status is more negative for black immigrants than for black natives in support of conflict theory's double disadvantage hypothesis. White immigrants are at parity with white natives in this preliminary model. Once educational differences between groups are controlled (model 2), the gap in occupational attainment between black and white natives virtually closes. That between black immigrants and white natives remains the same and cannot be explained away by compositional differences in human capital. As seen in both the U.S. and Canada, white immigrants have a significantly more positive labor market experience than black immigrants. In model 2, net of human capital, the white foreign-born do suffer an occupational setback relative to white natives, but this is less than that experienced by black immigrants.

The results for the black and white foreign-born remain the same in model 3 once other relevant labor market characteristics are controlled. However, black natives have a net occupational disadvantage relative to white natives. Interestingly, this disadvantage is not significantly different from that faced by white immigrants. So while race has a negative effect on occupational status, place of birth provides a significant advantage that allows black natives to compete with white natives at the same level as white immigrants. This allows both white immigrants and black natives to have adjusted mean occupational status scores that are almost at par with the scores of white natives (Table 7.7). This is similar to patterns observed for women in Canada where black natives and white immigrants with a duration of eleven to twenty years are at occupational parity with white natives. Unfortunately, the English results cannot be qualified by an examination of the effects of duration. As observed in other countries, black immigrants remain the most significantly disadvantaged of all groups of women in this study. Similar to Canada, education does not mitigate the effect of race-immigrant status on occupational attainment.

The relative positioning of men in the English occupational hierarchy closely parallels that of women (Table 7.6). Black natives have significantly lower occupational outcomes than white natives across models (models 1 to 3). Furthermore, black immigrants are doubly disadvantaged. For both black ethnic groups, some of the gap in occupational outcomes is attributable to differences in human capital. However, the effects of race and immigrant status remain significant net of relevant controls, in support of conflict theory. In a departure from the results for women, white male immigrants actually have occupational parity with their native counterparts and this pattern persists even when relevant labor market characteristics are controlled (model 3). Even though black natives are disadvantaged relative to white natives, the effect of race-immigrant status is not significantly different for black natives relative to white immigrants. An examination of adjusted mean status scores reveals that black natives come very close to parity with white natives. As with women, education has a positive effect on occupational attainment but does not, in addition, mitigate the effects of race-immigrant status.

Despite the similarity in overall patterns for men and women, foreign-born status has a greater negative effect for white women than for white men. However, no gender difference in occupational disadvantage is observed for black immigrants and natives. Thus, the conflict hypothesis of triple disadvantage is not supported despite evidence of gender inequality among whites. Furthermore, education is differentially rewarded on the basis of gender as observed in Canada and the U.S. The gender gap in returns to educational qualification is largest at the post-secondary level and narrows as qualifications increase. A postgraduate degree is rewarded with a 26-point increase in occupational status for men and a 22-point increase for women, relative to those without qualifications. Again, the gender gap in returns to human capital investment is smaller than in the U.S. Interestingly, while the gender gap in returns to education declines with increased qualifications in England, in the U.S. the gender gap actually widens as qualifications increase.

The results for England are a bit superficial given the lack of information on immigrant duration. However, there are similarities in results across country. For example, with the exception of black men in the U.S., in all three countries, the patterns for men and women reveal black native occupational advantage relative to black immigrants. In fact, (again with the exception of men in the U.S.), black natives are at or near occupational parity with white natives, net of relevant labor market characteristics. This outcome, however, is achieved with a unique interactive effect of education in the U.S. where the black native population is predominantly African-American rather than second-generation Caribbean. Black native advantage over black immigrants is often interpreted as evidence of double disadvantage for the latter when white immigrants also have an advantage. However, in Canada and England, where the black native population is predominantly second-generation Caribbean, black native advantage could also be interpreted as a long-term outcome of immigrant adaptation.

COMPARATIVE IMMIGRANT ADAPTATION AND SOCIO-POLITICAL CONTEXT

Overall, the patterns of occupational attainment vary by gender within country. There are also some general similarities in results across country despite notable specific differences. The remaining issue of interest is this: in which country do black immigrants have the most favorable outcomes? Could any of the observed differences in occupational outcomes across country be informed by national variation in socio-political context? This is really a structural issue. To what extent does mode of incorporation - conceptualized here as current and historical race relations, race relations policy, and immigration policy - inform outcomes for black immigrants? T-tests (results not shown) were done in order to determine whether the effect of race-immigrant status varied by country. Model 3 was used to compare regression results for Canada and the U.S. since the interactive model was significant only in the U.S. Model 2 was also used to compare regression results for all three countries since duration-specific status was not available in England.

An examination of the U.S.-Canada tests reveals that the effect of immigrant status does not differ significantly between countries where black men are concerned. Thus, black male immigrants would do equally well, or poorly, in either socio-political context even though those in the U.S. are significantly more highly educated than those in Canada (see Table 6.9). In tests involving England, patterns show that black foreign-born men have the worst outcomes in England while those for Canada and the U.S. are similar. These findings provide some support for the expectation that black immigrants will have the poorest outcomes in England. Black immigrant males are concentrated in skilled blue-collar jobs in each country. However, England's mode of incorporation - a more racially unfriendly socio-political context - may influence the poorer outcomes for black immigrant males compared with those in North America. On the other hand, the English economy is more industrialized, and West Indian men are concentrated in declining industrial jobs, which may provide an alternative explanation for observed patterns.

Surprisingly, black immigrant women have significantly worse outcomes in the U.S. than in Canada. This is true for immigrants at all levels of duration. These results are not attributable to poorer immigrant quality in the U.S. since, like men, black female immigrants in the U.S. are significantly more highly educated than those in Canada (see Table 6.8). It is possible that Canada's multicultural context, as opposed to the U.S.' assimilationist context, is currently more hospitable to immigrants despite historical similarities in hostility towards immigrants and in spite of civil rights and Affirmative Action legislation in the U.S. In fact, the practical applications of Affirmative Action to black immigrants are a topic of debate among scholars.

Another possible explanation may involve the way in which immigrants are drawn into the occupational hierarchies of each country. Thirty-three percent of black female immigrants work in service jobs (with only four percent in domestic jobs) in the U.S. economy. The comparable figure is sixteen percent in Canada (see Table 6.6). Both countries have made the transition to a technology- and knowledge-based economy dominated by service industries. In both countries, immigrants rank lowest in employers' labor queues relative to black natives, white immigrants, and white natives as earlier results of the relative positioning of groups imply. Yet, the U.S. and Canada differ dramatically in their utilization of immigrant labor and talent. Why?

One of the primary objectives of Canadian immigration policy has been nation-building, which in recent decades has been more inclusive of non-whites (Reitz, 1988). This has allowed Canada to be a primary beneficiary of brain-drain from developing countries, including those in the Caribbean (Palmer, 1995). Canada aggressively utilized skilled and professional immigrants, especially women, along with natives as it made its transition to a service economy (and to a welfare state with expanding social services). While the U.S. has also made this transition to a service economy, the key beneficiaries have been white native women whose increased educational attainment allowed them to move up employers' labor queues as white native men moved on to even better jobs. While black professional immigrants have also been recruited in response to labor demand in the U.S., black immigrants have been disproportionately pulled into the service economy to provide labor in support of native working women, particularly whites. Thus, while a significant proportion of black female immigrants are a part of the professional workforce in Canada as a result of the relative openness of the Canadian social hierarchy, in the U.S., a significant proportion of black female immigrants *support* the professional workforce, often in jobs that under-utilize or have nothing to do with their educational qualifications or previous labor market experience.

Tests involving England suggest that black female immigrants in Canada have the best outcomes followed by those in England, then those in the U.S. This positioning of the latter two countries is decidedly contrary to the expected since descriptive analyses suggest that inequality is greater in England. England also has a distinctively less hospitable climate for minorities and immigrants relative to North America, as reflected in immigration and race relations policies. Furthermore, female immigrants are even more concentrated in service jobs in the English economy than they are in the U.S. and far fewer have advanced education relative to those in the U.S.

Tests of significant difference in the effect of race-immigrant status by country were also done for natives. Black native men in the U.S. compare unfavorably to those in Canada. In addition, black native men in England do less well than those in Canada. The results for England are as expected given socio-political context. Furthermore, Canada may provide a more tolerant climate for black natives given its multicultural policies and the relative openness of social hierarchy that includes minorities and immigrants in its "nation-building." The result is a social hierarchy that is less rigidly race-based. This is supported by descriptive analyses that show lower levels of racial inequality in Canada's occupational hierarchy relative to the U.S. and England (Table 6.7).

The t-tests for women show that black natives have the worst outcomes in the U.S. (that is, the negative effect of black native status is largest in the U.S.) This is also true for men. These findings could reflect the stigma of slavery still attached to the African-American population (Hacker, 1992) since the black native population of the other two countries is largely of immigrant origin.

In summary, the socio-political context of countries may provide some insight into national differences in occupational outcomes of immigrants. However, other structural factors, such as the nature of the economy of receiving societies are also important. In fact, neo-Marxist structural theories (introduced in chapter 1) that focus on the nature of modern industrial economies and the specific ways in which immigrants are recruited into the occupational hierarchy of receiving economies in response to labor demand occasionally provide alternative explanations. It is important to note that economic context may influence socio-political context which may then influence economic context, and so on. They operate in tandem with one another to influence immigrants' outcomes.

It is possible, however, that the specific labor demands of a nation, along with the relative scarcity of skilled workers from a preferred group, may provide a more proximate determinant of labor market outcomes for immigrants.

Table 7.1: OLS Regression Analysis of ISEI for U.S. Women

Variables	Model 1	Model 2	Model 3 [a]	Model 4 [a]
Race-Immigrant Status:				
(White native - reference)				
Black native	-5.460***	-3.427***	----	----
Black foreign-born	-8.589***	-6.061***	----	----
White foreign-born	-1.337***	-0.994**	----	----
Educational Qualification: [b]				
(No post-sec. certif. - ref.)				
Post-sec. certif., no degree		7.877***	7.334***	3.932***
B.A.		14.905***	13.891***	10.656***
Graduate/Professional		20.802***	19.431***	16.853***
Race-immigrant				
Status/duration:				
(White native - reference)				
Black native			-4.256***	-6.409***
Black FB in U.S. 0-10 yrs			-8.619***	-11.30***
Black FB in U.S. 11-20 yrs			-6.067***	-9.398***
Black FB in U.S. > 20 yrs			-5.632***	-8.313***
White FB in U.S. 0-10 yrs			-3.977***	-4.540***
White FB in U.S. 11-20 yrs			-1.353**	-3.328***
White FB in U.S. > 20 yrs			0.650	-1.800**
Educ*Race-Immigrant				
Status/Duration:				
Bl. Native* Post-sec.				3.315***
Bl. Native* B.A.				4.508***
Bl. Native* G/P				5.414***
Bl. FB 0-10 yrs* Post-sec.				5.130***
Bl. FB 0-10 yrs* B.A.				6.617***
Bl. FB 0-10 yrs* G/P				-1.251
Bl. FB 11-20 yrs* Post-sec.				6.240***
Bl. FB 11-20 yrs* B.A.				6.136***
Bl. FB 11-20 yrs* G/P				2.240

Table 7.1 *continued*

Variables	Model 1	Model 2	Model 3 [a]	Model 4 [a]
Bl. FB > 20 yrs* Post-sec.				5.842***
Bl. FB > 20 yrs* B.A.				3.544**
Bl. FB > 20 yrs* G/P				1.276
Wh. FB 0-10 yrs* Post-sec.				0.816
Wh. FB 0-10 yrs* B.A.				2.631
Wh. FB 0-10 yrs* G/P				-0.161
Wh. FB 11-20 yrs* Post-sec.				3.926**
Wh. FB 11-20 yrs* B.A.				2.121
Wh. FB 11-20 yrs* G/P				3.144 +
Wh. FB > 20 yrs* Post-sec.				4.960***
Wh. FB > 20 yrs* B.A.				2.824*
Wh. FB > 20 yrs* G/P				4.076**
Y-intercept	52.206	43.787	43.304	45.167
Adjusted R^2	0.0629	0.2376	0.2570	0.2620
(df)	(5)	(8)	(23)	(44)
N=17,357				

* $p<.05$; ** $p<.01$; *** $p<.001$; + $p<.10$
[a] Model includes other independent variables and context controls defined in Table 5.2, as well as the sample selection correction factor, lambda. School attendance was dropped from the model due to non-significance.
[b] See Table 5.2 for definition of this variable.

Table 7.2: OLS Regression Analysis of ISEI for U.S. Men

Variables	Model 1	Model 2	Model 3 [a]	Model 4 [a]
Race-Immigrant Status:				
(White native - reference)				
Black native	-8.404***	-3.767***	----	----
Black foreign-born	-7.963***	-3.217***	----	----
White foreign-born	0.009	-0.194	----	----
Educational Qualification: [b]				
(No post-sec. certif. - ref.)				
Post-sec. certif., no degree		8.713***	8.350***	7.804***
B.A.		19.385***	18.891***	19.294***
Graduate/Professional		28.585***	27.770***	28.805***
Race-Immigrant				
Status/duration:				
(White native - reference)				
Black native			-3.693***	-3.829***
Black FB in U.S. 0-10 yrs			-3.952***	-3.789***
Black FB in U.S. 11-20 yrs			-3.077***	-3.049***
Black FB in U.S. > 20 yrs			-2.881***	-3.089***
White FB in U.S. 0-10 yrs			-1.049*	1.467+
White FB in U.S. 11-20 yrs			-1.092*	-0.656
White FB in U.S. > 20 yrs			0.337	-0.293
Educ*Race-Immigrant				
Status/Duration:				
Bl. Native* Post-sec.				0.339
Bl. Native* B.A.				1.048
Bl. Native* G/P				1.848
Bl. FB 0-10 yrs* Post-sec.				0.162
Bl. FB 0-10 yrs* B.A.				-0.409
Bl. FB 0-10 yrs* G/P				-1.229
Bl. FB 11-20 yrs* Post-sec.				0.176
Bl. FB 11-20 yrs* B.A.				1.169
Bl. FB 11-20 yrs* G/P				-1.295

Table 7.2 *continued*

Variables	Model 1	Model 2	Model 3 [a]	Model 4 [a]
Bl. FB > 20 yrs* Post-sec.				2.506*
Bl. FB > 20 yrs* B.A.				-3.278*
Bl. FB > 20 yrs* G/P				-0.631
Wh. FB 0-10 yrs* Post-sec.				-0.544
Wh. FB 0-10 yrs* B.A.				-5.373***
Wh. FB 0-10 yrs* G/P				-6.339***
Wh. FB 11-20 yrs* Post-sec.				1.281
Wh. FB 11-20 yrs* B.A.				-1.668
Wh. FB 11-20 yrs* G/P				-2.891*
Wh. FB > 20 yrs* Post-sec.				2.430*
Wh. FB > 20 yrs* B.A.				0.686
Wh. FB > 20 yrs* G/P				-0.376
Y-intercept	49.843	38.063	34.101	33.925
Adjusted R^2	0.0802	0.3706	0.3788	0.3808
(df)	(5)	(8)	(23)	(44)
N=16,488				

* $p<.05$; ** $p<.01$; *** $p<.001$; + $p<.10$

[a] Model includes other independent variables and context controls defined in Table 5.2, as well as the sample selection correction factor, lambda. School attendance was dropped from the model due to non-significance.

[b] See Table 5.2 for definition of this variable.

Table 7.3: OLS Regression Analysis of ISEI for Canadian Women

Variables	Model 1	Model 2	Model 3 [a]	Model 4 [a]
Race-Immigrant Status:				
(White native - reference)				
Black native	-0.396	-0.475	----	----
Black foreign-born	-3.638***	-2.910***	----	----
White foreign-born	0.887*	0.235	----	----
Educational Qualification: [b]				
(No post-sec. certif. - ref.)				
Post-sec. certif., no degree		4.977***	5.635***	4.870***
B.A./equivalent		11.000***	11.689***	11.825***
Graduate/Professional		16.670***	17.541***	16.057***
Race-Immigrant				
Status/duration:				
(White native - reference)				
Black native			-0.470	0.660
Black FB in U.S. 0-10 yrs			-4.170***	-5.388***
Black FB in U.S. 11-20 yrs			-2.410***	-4.147***
Black FB in U.S. > 20 yrs			-1.340*	-2.261*
White FB in U.S. 0-10 yrs			-1.881*	-2.153
White FB in U.S. 11-20 yrs			-0.834	-0.346
White FB in U.S. > 20 yrs			1.390**	1.390*
Educ*Race-Immigrant				
Status/Duration:				
Bl. Native* Post-sec.				-1.501
Bl. Native* B.A.				-3.802*
Bl. Native* G/P				0.693
Bl. FB 0-10 yrs* Post-sec.				2.539*
Bl. FB 0-10 yrs* B.A.				2.002
Bl. FB 0-10 yrs* G/P				-4.762
Bl. FB 11-20 yrs* Post-sec.				2.984**
Bl. FB 11-20 yrs* B.A.				0.427
Bl. FB 11-20 yrs* G/P				9.830*

Table 7.3 *continued*

Variables	Model 1	Model 2	Model 3 [a]	Model 4 [a]
Bl. FB 11-20 yrs* Post-sec.				2.984**
Bl. FB 11-20 yrs* B.A.				0.427
Bl. FB 11-20 yrs* G/P				9.830*
Bl. FB > 20 yrs* Post-sec.				1.151
Bl. FB > 20 yrs* B.A.				0.379
Bl. FB > 20 yrs* G/P				8.711*
Wh. FB 0-10 yrs* Post-sec.				0.477
Wh. FB 0-10 yrs* B.A.				-0.186
Wh. FB 0-10 yrs* G/P				-3.512
Wh. FB 11-20 yrs* Post-sec.				-0.429
Wh. FB 11-20 yrs* B.A.				-1.967
Wh. FB 11-20 yrs* G/P				1.493
Wh. FB > 20 yrs* Post-sec.				-0.146
Wh. FB > 20 yrs* B.A.				0.478
Wh. FB > 20 yrs* G/P				-1.376
Y-intercept	50.371	45.574	38.973	39.059
Adjusted R^2	0.0387	0.1705	0.1785	0.1822
(df)	(5)	(8)	(19)	(40)
N=5,167				

* p<.05; ** p<.01; *** p<.001; + p<.10
[a] Model includes independent variables and context controls defined in Table 5.2, as well as the sample selection correction factor, lambda. School attendance was dropped from model due to non-significance. Percent black and percent foreign were dropped due to high correlation with residence in Toronto.
[b] See Table 5.2 for definition of this variable.

Table 7.4: OLS Regression Analysis of ISEI for Canadian Men

Variables	Model 1	Model 2	Model 3 [a]	Model 4 [a]
Race-Immigrant Status:				
(White native - reference)				
Black native	0.192	0.184	----	----
Black foreign-born	-4.675***	-2.706***	----	----
White foreign-born	1.939***	1.072*	----	----
Educational Qualification: [b]				
(No post-sec. certif. - ref.)				
Post-sec. certif., no degree		4.554***	4.956***	4.785***
B.A./equivalent		15.042***	15.175***	15.073***
Graduate/Professional		20.116***	20.258***	18.687***
Race-Immigrant				
Status/duration:				
(White native - reference)				
Black native			-0.596	-0.648
Black FB in U.S. 0-10 yrs			-4.454***	-4.467***
Black FB in U.S. 11-20 yrs			-3.246***	-3.768***
Black FB in U.S. > 20 yrs			-3.342***	-3.987**
White FB in U.S. 0-10 yrs			1.078	1.643
White FB in U.S. 11-20 yrs			-0.501	1.001
White FB in U.S. > 20 yrs			1.081*	0.250
Educ*Race-Immigrant				
Status/Duration:				
Bl. Native* Post-sec.				0.760
Bl. Native* B.A.				-1.254
Bl. Native* G/P				-3.893
Bl. FB 0-10 yrs* Post-sec.				-0.408
Bl. FB 0-10 yrs* B.A.				-0.650
Bl. FB 0-10 yrs* G/P				10.435*
Bl. FB 11-20 yrs* Post-sec.				0.443
Bl. FB 11-20 yrs* B.A.				4.123+
Bl. FB 11-20 yrs* G/P				1.059

Table 7.4 *continued*

Variables	Model 1	Model 2	Model 3 [a]	Model 4 [a]
Bl. FB > 20 yrs* Post-sec.				0.201
Bl. FB > 20 yrs* B.A.				1.473
Bl. FB > 20 yrs* G/P				7.548*
Wh. FB 0-10 yrs* Post-sec.				-0.525
Wh. FB 0-10 yrs* B.A.				-1.669
Wh. FB 0-10 yrs* G/P			.	1.234
Wh. FB 11-20 yrs* Post-sec.				-2.100
Wh. FB 11-20 yrs* B.A.				-2.262
Wh. FB 11-20 yrs* G/P				-0.592
Wh. FB > 20 yrs* Post-sec.				1.098
Wh. FB > 20 yrs* B.A.				0.935
Wh. FB > 20 yrs* G/P				2.463
Y-intercept	46.681	40.322	23.247	23.896
Adjusted R^2	0.0565	0.2250	0.2309	0.2307
(df)	(5)	(8)	(19)	(40)
N=5,030				

* $p<.05$; ** $p<.01$; *** $p<.001$; + $p<.10$

[a] Model includes independent variables and context controls defined in Table 5.2, as well as the sample selection correction factor, lambda. School attendance was dropped from model due to non-significance. Percent black and percent foreign were dropped due to high correlation with residence in Toronto.

[b] See Table 5.2 for definition of this variable.

Table 7.5: OLS Regression Analysis of ISEI for British Women

Variables	Model 1	Model 2	Model 3 [a]	Model 4 [a]
Race-Immigrant Status:				
(White native - reference)				
Black native	-2.197***	-0.939+	-1.752**	-1.133+
Black foreign-born	-5.502***	-4.743***	-5.774***	-5.772***
White foreign-born	0.009	-1.343*	-2.203**	-1.941**
Educational Qualification: [b]				
(No post-sec. certif. - ref.)				
Post-sec. certif., no degree		9.870***	8.925***	11.362***
B.A. equivalent		18.525***	16.995***	17.585***
Graduate/Professional		22.725***	21.550***	22.610***
Educ*Race-Immigrant Status				
Bl. Native* Post-sec.				-4.935*
Bl. Native* B.A.				-4.192*
Bl. Native* G/P				-13.372+
Bl. FB* Post-sec.				-2.046
Bl. FB* B.A.				4.322
Bl. FB* G/P				4.923
Wh. FB* Post-sec.				-2.305+
Wh. FB* B.A.				-0.420
Wh. FB* G/P				-0.737
Y-intercept	46.779	43.223	40.286	40.118
Adjusted R^2	0.1017	0.2605	0.2850	0.2867
(df)	(5)	(8)	(20)	(29)
N=4,220				

* p<.05; ** p<.01; *** p<.001; + p<.10
[a] Model includes independent variables and context controls defined in Table 5.2, as well as the sample selection correction factor, lambda.
[b] See Table 5.2 for definition of this variable.

114

Table 7.6: OLS Regression Analysis of ISEI for British Men

Variables	Model 1	Model 2	Model 3 [a]	Model 4 [a]
Race-Immigrant Status:				
(White native - reference)				
Black native	-4.319***	-1.416*	-1.444*	-0.999
Black foreign-born	-7.173***	-4.440***	-4.575***	-4.770***
White foreign-born	0.315	-0.561	-0.736	-0.957
Educational Qualification: [b]				
(No post-sec. certif. - ref.)				
Post-sec. certif., no degree		14.585***	14.552***	15.611***
B.A. equivalent		21.742***	21.506***	20.824***
Graduate/Professional		25.824***	25.464***	26.473***
Educ*Race-Immigrant Status				
Bl. Native* Post-sec.				-5.012+
Bl. Native* B.A.				-5.699*
Bl. Native*Post B.A.				-4.152
Bl. FB* Post-sec.				-1.417
Bl. FB* B.A.				7.989*
Bl. FB* Post B.A.				4.465
Wh. FB* Post-sec.				0.491
Wh. FB* B.A.				2.434
Wh. FB* Post B.A.				-2.207
Y-intercept	45.092	40.260	31.845	31.572
Adjusted R^2	0.0715	0.3100	0.3177	0.3201
(df)	(5)	(8)	(20)	(29)
N=4,049				

*p<.05; ** p<.01; *** p<.001; + p<.10

[a] Model includes independent variables and context controls defined in Table 5.2, as well as the sample selection correction factor, lambda.

[b] See Table 5.2 for definition of this variable.

Table 7.7: Country- and Gender-specific Adjusted Mean Occupational Status Scores: by race-immigrant status, duration and educational qualification

Race-immigrant status by duration and educational qualification	The U.S.		Canada [a]		England [a, b]	
	Wom.	Men	Wom.	Men	Wom.	Men
White native:						
No qualification	46	38	45	41	42	40
Post-secondary	50	46	50	45	51	55
B.A. or equivalent	57	57	56	56	59	62
Graduate/Professional	63	67	62	61	64	66
Black native:						
No qualification	40	34	44 (ns)	40 (ns)	41	39
Post-secondary	47	42	50 (ns)	45 (ns)	49	53
B.A. or equivalent	55	54	56 (ns)	55 (ns)	58	60
Graduate/Professional	62	63	62 (ns)	60 (ns)	62	64
Black immigr. 0-10 yrs.[b]						
No qualification	35	34	41	36	37	36
Post-secondary	44	42	46	41	45	50
B.A. or equivalent	52	54	52	51	54	57
Graduate/Professional	52	63	58	56	58	61
Black immigrant 11-20 yrs.						
No qualification	37	35	42	37	--	--
Post-secondary	47	43	48	42	--	--
B.A. or equivalent	54	54	54	52	--	--
Graduate/Professional	53	64	60	58	--	--
Black immigrant > 20 yrs.						
No qualification	37	35	43	37	--	--
Post-secondary	48	45	49	42	--	--
B.A. or equivalent	52	51	55	52	--	--
Graduate/Professional	55	64	61	57	--	--

Table 7.7 *continued*

Race-immigrant status by duration and educational qualification	The U.S.		Canada [a]		England [a, b]	
	Wom.	Men	Wom.	Men	Wom.	Men
White immigr. 0-10 yrs.[b]						
No qualification	42	40	43	42 (ns)	40	40 (ns)
Post-secondary	46	47	48	47 (ns)	49	54 (ns)
B.A. or equivalent	52	54	55	57 (ns)	57	61 (ns)
Graduate/Professional	58	62	60	62 (ns)	62	65 (ns)
White immigrant 11-20 yrs						
No qualification	43	37 (ns)	44 (ns)	40 (ns)	--	–
Post-secondary	51	45 (ns)	50 (ns)	45 (ns)	--	–
B.A. or equivalent	53	57 (ns)	56 (ns)	55 (ns)	--	–
Graduate/Professional	60	63	61 (ns)	60 (ns)	–	–
White immigrant > 20 yrs.						
No qualification	44	38 (ns)	46	42	--	–
Post-secondary	53	48	52	47	--	–
B.A. or equivalent	58	57 (ns)	58	57	--	–
Graduate/Professional	65	67 (ns)	64	62	–	–

[a] Adjusted means were calculated using model 3 (additive model of best fit for these countries) rather than model 4, the interactive model of best fit for the U.S.
[b] No duration information is available for England. Thus, adjusted means are provided for the **general** sample of black and white immigrants.
[ns] Not significantly different from reference group (white natives).

CHAPTER 8

Summary and Conclusion

Race, immigrant status and gender are three major dimensions of social stratification. While it has been established that being minority, immigrant or female places people at a disadvantage in the labor market, the confluence of these statuses has been largely ignored in analytic models of immigrant adaptation. I address this shortcoming by examining interactive models of occupational attainment, with a focus on the role that education plays in counteracting disadvantage, over and above that observed on average (in additive models). I situate this issue in the context of Caribbean adaptation research.

Until recently, the focus of such research has been to examine whether or not black immigrants have better economic outcomes than black natives. In the U.S. this is an important question because of the implications for race-based social programs and policies. To what extent is discrimination a factor in the relative outcomes of black natives? Is race more important that ethnicity? In other words, what does it mean for one black ethnic group to have more favorable socioeconomic outcomes relative to another? Any observed immigrant advantage has, so far, been attributed to cultural superiority, immigrant selectivity, and employer favoritism.

Researchers have since adopted a cross-national approach as a means of testing the soundness of current theoretical explanations being applied to U.S. findings. So far, the cultural superiority argument has been debunked. In addition, Dodoo (1997) makes a convincing case against immigrant selectivity as the primary reason for observed immigrant-native differences in labor market outcomes. While descriptive analyses support previous findings of immigrant advantage in education and (unadjusted) mean occupational status for men, my multivariate research findings cannot inform these focused theoretical debates because findings do not confirm significant immigrant advantage in occupational attainment for men or women, net of relevant factors.

Regardless of which black ethnic group does better, both do less well relative to white natives - according to previous research. I advance the scholarship on Caribbean immigrant adaptation by examining the extent to which education mitigates combinations of disadvantaged statuses. More specifically, I model the interaction of race, immigrant status and education on the occupational attainment of men and women. Black Caribbean immigrants are compared with black natives and white natives for continuity with previous research. They are also compared with white immigrants, who function as a control group.

Since Caribbean immigrants tend to migrate most heavily to the U.S., Canada, and - in the recent past - England, an examination of Caribbean immigrants' adaptation outcomes involves an analysis of all three countries. Chapter 1 provides an overview of the migration experiences of Caribbean immigrants and places them in the context of international migration theories. This provides insight into the ways in which immigrants become situated in the labor market hierarchy of receiving societies. Of importance to the comparison of their occupational outcomes relative to those of black natives is a bridging of both the race relations and immigrant adaptation literatures. Historical and current race relations may impact outcomes for non-white immigrants, hence the attention given to the experiences of native minorities. Likewise, hostility towards immigrants - often reflected in immigration policies - may have repercussions for the labor market experience of immigrants. Thus, the second major issue is the extent to which the socio-political context of receiving countries, as defined by race relations policy and immigration policy, informs immigrants' outcomes. Socio-political context is conceptualized as part of the 'mode of incorporation' or receptivity to immigrants mentioned by Portes and others.

Key theoretical positions, derived from the review of theories of international migration, immigrant adaptation, and minority incorporation, are summarized in Table 8.1 along with key findings. How do the occupational outcomes of black immigrants compare to those of white and black natives as well as white immigrants? How are results different or similar for men and women? And how do results vary across country? In general, no one theoretical approach provides all the answers. Instead, they each contribute to the understanding of immigrants' experiences.

In support of neo-classical economic/straight-line assimilation theory, there is an initial disadvantage of immigrant status for women in the U.S. and Canada. Duration of time in receiving society functions to decrease disadvantage over time. For men, the results are less clear cut. Black immigrants do start off with an initial immigrant disadvantage in the U.S. and Canada. However, duration has a very limited assimilation effect for black men. White immigrants provide a contrast for black immigrants. On average, they do have an initial occupational disadvantage relative to white natives, but tend to achieve parity with or occupational advantage over white natives with time in receiving country (U.S. men and women, Canadian women). In Canada, white immigrant men actually have initial *parity* with white native men, and immigrant advantage after twenty years. Also in support of neo-classical theory, education does significantly increase occupational attainment in all three countries. However, more in support of conflict perspective, rewards to education vary by group.

Neo-Marxist theoretical expectations are divided into conflict and structural positions. Conflict theory expects that minorities or immigrants, as a function of neo-colonial labor exploitation, will be poorly educated relative to white natives, with severely limited chances for upward mobility. While this may be true for immigrants with low skills and little education, not everyone is doomed to occupy the lowest-status occupations. Rather, in support of ethnic stratification and segmentation theory, immigrants are initially positioned at various levels of the occupational hierarchy. This is often a result of diversity of human capital characteristics. Descriptive analyses provide support for occupational niching and entrepreneurship among immigrants.

Other conflict expectations are supported. In all three countries, there is evidence of the double disadvantage of race and immigrant status for women. Black native women have higher adjusted occupational status outcomes than immigrants. Among men, double disadvantage is true only among Canadian and English men. In the U.S., the occupational outcomes of black immigrant and native men are not significantly different. There is an additional expectation of triple disadvantage where black immigrant women are expected to compare less favorably relative to black immigrant (and indirectly relative to white men). There is some evidence of this in the U.S. and only very weak support of this in Canada. While the specific nature of the effect of race varies cross-nationally, overall, race does matter in each country, as do immigrant status (with the exception of black men in the U.S.) and gender.

The neo-Marxist structural argument takes into account larger contextual factors, such as economic restructuring, discrimination, and mode of incorporation, that may affect immigrants' outcomes. In all three countries, racial minorities and immigrants tend to be concentrated in lower-status jobs relative to whites. They are also geographically concentrated in regions or areas of cities that have high unemployment due to changes in the manufacturing industry (see, for example, Cross, 1992; Henry, 1994; Hamnett and Randolph, 1994; Wilson, 1996). In theory, human capital is key to allowing immigrants to achieve occupational mobility in economies that undergo restructuring. In each country, the loss of industrial jobs due to economic restructuring was particularly detrimental to minority men because of their higher concentration in blue-collar jobs (see, for example, Cross, 1992; Owen, 1997; Green, 1997; Sassen, 1995). Given the transformation to information-based and technology-driven economies, minorities and newer non-white immigrants need to invest in human capital in order to remain viable in today's labor market. Racial discrimination also affects the labor market outcomes of minorities, including immigrants.

To what extent does education mitigate the negative effects of race and immigrant status for men and women? Is the mitigating effect different in each country? Education is expected to have not only main effects but also interactive effects that counteract race-immigrant status. Interestingly, interactive models are significant only in the U.S. Furthermore, education is more effective at mitigating race-immigrant status for women than men. It is possible that qualifications are more effective in counteracting race-immigrant status because the U.S. is a more credential society than Canada and England.

Furthermore, the U.S. has a larger managerial layer than Canada so that there is a higher premium on education (Esping-Andersen, 1993). As natives advance in employers' labor queues in the ever-expanding U.S. economy, education becomes an important tool for immigrants and minorities to advance into lower-status white-collar jobs. Women are at a particular advantage in the new post-industrial economy. As more women have entered the workforce, the welfare state has expanded to provide more social services. This in turn creates more jobs for women (Esping-Andersen, 1993) as the state assumes more and more of the functions of the traditional family.

Does variation in national socio-political context inform cross-national differences in the occupational outcomes of immigrants? To some extent, as observed with the U.S. and Canada. For example, despite very similar economies, Canada has a more tolerant socio-political climate and a more open social hierarchy so that the effects of immigrant status are often better relative to the U.S. However, there are alternative structural explanations for national differences in occupational outcomes for immigrants.

As economies are transformed over time, immigrants' outcomes may be influenced not only by the social climate created by national policies, but also by the specific nature of social characteristics and economic change in each country. For example, England has a less friendly socio-political climate and is associated with worst case outcomes for black immigrant men. However, England's economy is still very industrial relative to those in North America. England also happens to have an economy that is very open at the bottom of the social hierarchy but closed at the top (Esping-Andersen, 1993). Therefore, immigrants will find it easier to have jobs at the lower end of the social hierarchy. They are also less likely to be educated in distinguished schools, and quality of schooling is sufficient credential for later access to advantageous social positions even without a university degree (Muller et al, 1990; pg. 80). Few people actually even pursue advanced degrees since a general education is sufficient for career advancement (Muller et al, 1990). In addition, it is speculated that education, rather than being a social leveler in England, functions to promote social class divisions by blocking mobility into elite positions for all but the already advantaged (Gershuny, 1993). Thus, the socioeconomic context is as important as the socio-political in impacting immigrants' socioeconomic outcomes and experiences. Furthermore, the labor market experiences of women and men may be differentially impacted by structural factors (socio-political and economic).

What explains the general similarity in occupational experiences and outcomes across country? Overall, all three countries have made a transition from a manufacturing to a service-based economy, albeit at different rates, with England lagging behind North America. Similar low-skill and high-skill labor demands have allowed similar patterns of recruitment and placement of immigrants despite differences in socio-political context. This is reflected in Tables 6.6 and 6.7 which show that groups tend to occupy the same occupational categories in each country. However, as previously illustrated with the U.S. and Canada, occupational experiences for immigrants and minorities may still vary if countries utilize recruited labor differently. Black immigrant (and native) women in the U.S. are more highly educated than their Canadian counterparts, yet a smaller proportion of them are drawn into the professional occupations, relative to their Canadian counterparts.

What are some additional factors that may impact cross-national differences in immigrants' labor market outcomes besides occupational attainment? How may these and other factors impact immigrants' general chances for success in the post-industrial economies of receiving societies? And what changes can we expect to see in the future that may have repercussions for the labor market outcomes of immigrants and minorities? Unionization, technological changes, and demographic turnover in the labor force are key issues that will shape or continue to shape the economic trajectories of immigrants and minorities within the next few years.

First, Reitz (1998) suggests that unionization may be important for understanding cross-national differences in immigrants' economic outcomes. In general, immigrants are less likely than natives to have union membership. In some cities, they are also concentrated in peripheral jobs that are less likely to be unionized and more likely to be low-paying. Presumably, unionization increases the bargaining power of workers against employers, allowing for improved wages, work conditions, and benefits. Thus, unionization is part of the institutional context of immigrant economic adaptation in each receiving society, having implications for wages, employment stability, and quality of work life.

Researchers note some interesting cross-national patterns. The bargaining power of labor against capital is weaker in the U.S. than in England or Canada (Reitz, 1998; Myles et al, 1993). Furthermore, Canadian unions have been more receptive to immigrants than American ones (Reitz, 1998), and immigrants to Canada tend to be concentrated in areas of high unionization. Even if these immigrants were not union members, they would still have a wage benefit because strong union presence, across several labor market sectors, may positively impact the wages of both union and nonunion workers (Reitz, 1998). Not surprisingly, then, Reitz finds some evidence in support of higher immigrant wages in Canada relative to the U.S. The implication here is that immigrants to the U.S. may benefit from greater union membership. On the other hand, unions have been slowly losing their bargaining power, especially as the manufacturing base - a source of traditional union membership - has declined in each country (Myles et al, 1993; Cross, 1992). The diminishing power of unions is a factor in the wage declines noted among workers in traditional industrial occupations (Jacobs, 1993; Danziger and Gottschalk, 1995). Therefore, the beneficial effect of union membership on immigrants' wages may yet depend on how successful unions are in rejuvenating themselves and replenishing flagging membership with workers from non-traditional economic sectors.

Technological change, at the heart of industrial restructuring, is a second factor that will continue to profoundly impact the labor market outcomes of immigrants and minorities. The high-tech industry demands a highly-educated, highly-skilled workforce. In the U.S., labor demand in this industry has outpaced labor supply in recent years, such that employers have heavily recruited labor, especially from Asia and the Middle-East, in order to fill jobs. So high was the demand for this labor, that the annual limits on H-1B visas for non-immigrant working professionals were raised several times in the past few years. While H-1B visas are temporary, workers may eventually change their immigrant status to a more permanent one. This has implications for even greater segmentation of the labor market and rising inequality due to further bifurcation of wages, especially among immigrants. Assuming that labor demand continues to be high in this industry for several more years, black immigrants and natives have much to gain from capitalizing on this demand. Higher educational attainment and skills will prevent them from being shut out of highly-paid jobs in the U.S., Canada or England. Furthermore, it is possible that their chances of achieving upward mobility will increase as employers' tastes for race of employee give way to market demand.

Finally, demographic trends may impact the mobility chances of immigrants in the next fifteen to twenty-five years. As Baby Boomers leave the labor market, demand for labor in high- to mid-level jobs, across different economic sectors, may exceed supply. This would clear the way for settled immigrants, minorities, and some recent arrivals (depending on skill) to advance up the social hierarchy. On the other hand, unemployment would decline in the low-end service sector since the retirement of Boomers would increase demand for more elderly services.

Table 8.1: Tabular Summary of Multivariate Findings by Theoretical Expectations*

Theory	Theoretical Positions/Expectations	Supported? U.S.		Can.		UK	
		F	M	F	M	F	M
Neo-Classical Economic/ Straight-line Assimilation	A. initial disadvantage of immigrant status;	Y	R	Y	R	-	-
	- decreases with duration of time in receiving society (improved host-country-specific labor force experience and job skills)	Y	R	Y	R	-	-
	B. human capital has positive effect on occupational attainment;	Y	Y	Y	Y	Y	Y
	- no expectation of disparate rewards to qualification by race/ethnicity and gender	N	N	N	N	N	N
Neo-Marxist Labor Exploitation/ Conflict	A. racial minorities and non-white immigrants concentrated in lowest-status occupations with severely limited chances for upward mobility	R	R	R	R	R	R
	B. double oppression: negative effect of race and immigrant status	Y	N	Y	Y	Y	Y
	C. triple oppression: negative effects of race, immigrant status and gender	Y	-	R	-	N	-

127

Table 8.1 *continued*

Theory	Theoretical Positions/Expectations	Supported?					
		U.S.		Can.		UK	
		F	M	F	M	F	M
Neo-Marxist Structural	A. racial minorities and non-white immigrants concentrated in lower-status occupations with upward mobility conditional on human capital, especially given economic restructuring	Y	Y	Y	Y	Y	Y
	---> Education mitigates the negative effects of race and immigrant status (interactive effect)	Y	R	N	N	N	N
	B. discrimination -> rewards to human capital vary by race/ethnicity and gender	Y	Y	Y	Y	Y	Y
	C. mode of incorporation (socio-political context) impacts immigrant outcomes	R	R	R	R	R	R

Table 8.1 *continued*

Theory	Theoretical Positions/Expectations	Supported?					
		U.S.		Can.		UK	
		F	M	F	M	F	M
Ethnic Strat. & Segmentation/ Segmented Assimilation	A. specialization and discrimination –> occupational niching	Y	Y	Y	Y	Y	Y
	B. entrepreneurship	Y	Y	Y	Y	Y	Y
	C. ethnic enclaves	-	-	-	-	-	-
	D. diversity of human capital among immigrants resulting in diversity of <u>initial</u> positioning in social hierarchy	Y	Y	Y	Y	Y	Y

* F = women; M = men; R = Mixed results; - = Not applicable

Appendix

Table A.1: Preliminary OLS Regression Analysis of ISEI - U.S.

Variables	Model 1 [a]	Model 2	Model 3	Model 4
Age	0.064***	0.043***	0.026***	-0.015*
Age squared	-0.010***	-0.011***	-0.011***	-0.002***
Black	-7.076***	-7.262***	-7.056***	-3.685***
Gender (1=male)	-2.342***	-2.863***	-2.821***	-3.092***
Foreign-born	-1.382***	-1.085***	----	----
Duration of time in the U.S.				
0-10 years	-3.676***		-2.534***	-2.188***
11-20 years	-1.285***		-0.601*	-0.606**
> 20 years	0.911***		0.062	0.363
Educational Qualification: [b]				
(No post-sec. certif. - ref.)				
Post-sec. certif., no degree	8.942***			8.341***
B.A. equivalent	18.261***			17.166***
Graduate/Professional	26.387***			25.319***
Y-intercept		52.679	52.552	42.493
Adjusted R^2		0.0676	0.0696	0.3046
(df)		(5)	(7)	(10)
N=33,846				

*p<.05; ** p<.01; *** p<.001; + p<.10
[a] Model 1 is the bivariate model.
[b] See Table 5.2 for definition of this variable.

Table A.2: Preliminary OLS Regression Analysis of ISEI - Canada

Variables	Model 1 [a]	Model 2	Model 3	Model 4
Age	0.111***	0.098***	0.080***	0.043***
Age squared	-0.007***	-0.006***	-0.007***	-0.001
Black	-3.771***	-3.564***	-3.036***	-1.795***
Gender (1=male)	-3.487***	-3.717***	-3.721***	-4.178***
Foreign-born	-0.316	-0.543***	----	----
Duration of time in Canada				
0-10 years	-2.907***		-2.115***	-1.825***
11-20 years	-1.567***		-1.334***	-1.080***
> 20 years	1.749***		0.755*	0.527+
Educational Qualification: [b]				
(No post-sec. certif. - ref.)				
Post-sec. certif., no degree	4.958***			4.828***
B.A. equivalent	13.724***			13.292***
Graduate/Professional	19.523***			19.011***
Y-intercept		51.242	51.148	45.389
Adjusted R^2		0.0556	0.0600	0.2141
(df)		(5)	(7)	(10)
N=10,197				

*p<.05; ** p<.01; *** p<.001; + p<.10
[a] Model 1 is the bivariate model.
[b] See Table 5.2 for definition of this variable.

132

Table A.3: Preliminary OLS Regression Analysis of ISEI - England

Variables	Model 1 [a]	Model 2	Model 3
Age	-0.113***	-0.103***	-0.088***
Age squared	-0.013***	-0.012***	-0.007***
Black	-4.518***	-4.682***	-2.422***
Gender (1=male)	-1.693***	-1.527***	-1.332***
Foreign-born	-2.919***	-1.318***	-1.985***
Educational Qualification: [b]			
(No post-sec. certif. - ref.)			
Post-sec. certif., no degree	11.960**		11.261***
B.A. equivalent	21.924***		20.185***
Graduate/Professional	25.490**		24.902***
Y-intercept		47.174	42.833
Adjusted R^2		0.0820	0.2790
(df)		(5)	(8)
N=8,269			

*p<.05; ** p<.01; *** p<.001; + p<.10
[a] Model 1 is the bivariate model. Note that duration is not available in the British census data.
[b] See Table 5.2 for definition of this variable.

133

Notes

1. The "(Anglophone/British) Caribbean" and "West Indies" are terms used interchangeably to refer to those countries in the Caribbean which are current, or were former, territories of Britain. Residents of these countries, and immigrants with origins in these countries, are English-speaking and may be referred to as Caribbean, British Caribbean, Anglophone Caribbean or West Indian in this book. Countries include: Belize (British Honduras), Anguilla, Antigua and Barbuda, Bahamas, Barbados, British Virgin Islands, Cayman Islands, Dominica, Grenada, Jamaica, Montserrat, St. Barthelemy, St. Kitts-Nevis, St. Lucia, St. Vincent and the Grenadines, Trinidad and Tobago, Turks and Caicos Islands, and Guyana. Also included: Not specified - Caribbean, West Indies, Antilles, British West Indies, Leeward Islands, and Windward Islands. Because of their colonial history, these islands have socio-political, cultural and migratory experiences that are distinct from those of French-, Dutch- or Spanish-speaking islands.
2. Southern, Western and foreign sites provide cheap(er), non-unionized labor and some shelter from business taxes. De-industrialization occurred in part as a response to economic competition stemming from an increase in imported consumer and capital goods (see Gober, 1993) and to automation (Danziger and Gottschalk, 1995).
3. Innovations due to competitive pressure and the availability of new technologies generated increased demand for highly-skilled workers and contributed to job growth in high-tech, high-skill sectors of the economy (Portes and Zhou, 1992). At the same time, the expansion of the service sector generated increased demand for low-skill service workers.
4. "Unassimilable" colonials were those who did not fit the mold of what it meant to be "British." "Britishness" and rights of citizenship were determined by British birthplace or specific ancestry (regardless of place of residence) - which automatically selected out most non-whites. Irish colonials, incidentally, were never considered to be "unassimilable" (Carter et al., 1996).
5. To remove the confounding effects of English-language ability on attainment outcomes for white immigrants, the decision was made to equalize the white and black immigrant samples on this variable. Furthermore, there was insufficient variation on English-speaking ability to include it as an independent variable: 99.7%, 99.6%, and 99.1% of white natives, black natives, and Caribbean immigrants respectively reported that they were native speakers of English or that they could "speak English well/very well" (as opposed to "not very well" or "not at all"). In contrast, 10% of white immigrants could not speak English at all or did not speak it very well. This subset of white foreign-born was deleted from the analysis. Preliminary analyses were done with and without them. The results

show a stronger negative effect of immigrant status on occupational attainment in the models including white immigrants with very poor English language ability.

6.   In the U.S., Black Caribbean-born immigrants were those people who indicated that they were born in the West Indies (see endnote 1) and who identified themselves as "black" racially, and "non-Hispanic" ethnically.

7.   In the UK, immigrants were defined as black Caribbean-born if they indicated that their ethnic group was "Black Caribbean" or "Black Other" and they also selected "Jamaica" or "Other Caribbean Commonwealth" as their country of birth.   See endnote 1 for a listing of countries in the Caribbean Commonwealth.

8.   In Canada, Black Caribbean-born immigrants were defined as those who were born in "Central America, Caribbean and Bermuda, and South America," claimed Black/Caribbean origins, and were classified as visible minorities. They, as well as other sampled groups, selected English as their mother tongue.

9.   While Heckman's first-stage equation uses maximum likelihood probity under the assumption of normal distribution of error terms, Blau (1985) uses a first-stage logit model since "the normal and logistic distribution functions are quite similar" (pg. 355). See Blau (1985) for the exact specification of lambda.

10.   Traditionally, SEI indices have been constructed on the basis of the characteristics of male workers. Stevens and Featherman (1981) were the first to develop scales based on the attributes of both male and female workers.

11.   High-wage service industries include: transportation, communication and public utilities, wholesale trade, finance, real estate, insurance, professional services, and public administration.

12.   Only geographic areas with at least 60 Caribbean immigrants were selected for analyses (see chapter 5). Thus, these results are applicable to areas of high Caribbean concentration and inapplicable to areas with very few West Indians (see Ko and Clogg, 1986).

13.   For the U.S. sample, adjusted mean occupational status score = $B_0 + B_1$(mean age) + B_2(mean of age^2) + B_3(post-sec. certificate) + B_4 (B.A.) + B_5(graduate/prof.) + B_6(black native) + B_7(black FB 0-10 yrs) + B_8(black FB 11-20 yrs) + ... + B_{13}(proportion of sample married) + B_{14}(proportion of sample in public sector) + B_{15}(proportion of sample self-employed) + B_{16}(mean lambda) + B_{17}(black native*post-sec) + B_{18}(black native*BA) + ... + B_{37}(white FB >20 yrs*grad/prof) + B_i (mean of context control variable X_i). This equation is based on model 4, the interactive model of best fit for the U.S.   For the UK and Canadian sample, adjusted means were calculated from model 3, the additive model of best fit for these countries. The UK equations do not have duration-specific interaction terms, and those for both the UK and Canada do not have terms for public sector worker.   The Canadian models have only a subset of the context controls (see notes below Tables 7.3 and 7.4).   Adjusted means are summarized in Table 7.7.

14. It is interesting to note that while women's returns to education are lower than those of men, and that the effects of race-immigrant status are significantly worse for black women than for black men, mean adjusted scores for black men are sometimes lower than those for black women (Table 7.7, the U..S). This may be a function of men's greater concentration in blue-collar jobs relative to women's concentration in lower-status, white-collar jobs. Interestingly, in the U.S., at the graduate or professional level of education, where involvement in blue-collar jobs is very unlikely, black men's mean occupational status scores tend to be higher than women's scores.

15. As observed in the U.S., mean adjusted status scores for Canadian men are lower than those of women, possibly because men are more likely to be in blue-collar jobs. Note that adjusted means are not used as the focus of cross-national comparisons of occupational attainment or even of gender differences in labor market outcomes. Rather, emphasis is placed on comparing the effects of variables across country or across group within country with the use of t-tests.

References

Agresti, Alan and Barbara Finlay. 1986. *Statistical Methods for the Social Sciences.* 2nd edition. San Francisco: Dellen Publishing Company.

Anderton, Douglas L. and Deborah E. Sellers. 1993. "A Brief Review of Contextual-Effect Models and Measurement." Pg. 22-31in chapter 23 of *Readings in Population Research Methodology* vol. 6. Published by the Social Development Center, Chicago, IL for the United Nations Population Fund.

Anthias, Floya and Nira Yuval-Davis. 1992. *Racialized Boundaries: Race, Nation Gender, Colour and Class and the Anti-Racist Struggle.* London and New York: Routledge.

Berk, Richard. 1983. "An Introduction to Sample Selection Bias in Sociological Data." *American Sociological Review* 48 (June): 386-398.

Bilsborrow, Richard E. and Hania Zlotnick. 1994. "The Systems Approach and the Measurement of the Determinants of International Migration." Paper presented at the Workshop on Root Causes of International Migration. Luxembourg: Eurostat.

Blau, David M. 1985. "Self-Employment and Self-Selection in Developing Country Labor Markets." *Southern Economic Journal* 52(2): 351-363.

Bolaria, B. Singh and Peter S. Li (editors). 1988. *Racial Oppression in Canada.* Enlarged 2nd edition. Toronto: Garamond Press.

Borjas, George. 1991. "Immigration Policy, National Origin, and Immigrant Skills: A Comparison of Canada and the United States." National Bureau of Economic Research. vol. 28(2). Working Paper no. 3691.

Boyd, Monica. 1989. "Family and Personal Networks in International Migration: Recent Developments and New Agendas." *International Migration Review* 23: 638-670.

Brettell, Caroline B. and Rita James Simon. 1986. Ch. 1 in *International Migration: The Female Experience.* Edited by Caroline Brettell and Rita James Simon. New Jersey: Rowman and Allanheld.

Bureau of the Census. 1992a. Census of Population and Housing, 1990: Public Use Microdata Samples U.S. (machine-readable data files). Washington, DC.

Bureau of the Census. 1992b. Census of Population and Housing, 1990: Public Use Microdata Sample U.S. Technical Documentation. Washington, DC.

Bureau of the Census. 1992c. Census of Population and Housing, 1990: Summary Tape File 3 on CD-ROM. Washington, DC.

140   References

Bureau of the Census. 1992d. Census of Population and Housing, 1990: Summary Tape File 3 on CD-ROM. Technical Documentation. Washington, DC.

Butcher, Kristin F. 1994. "Black Immigrants in the United States: A Comparison with Native Blacks and Other Immigrants." *Industrial and Labor Relations Review* 47(2): 265-284.

Carter, Bob, Marci Green and Rick Halpern. 1996. "Immigration Policy and the Racialization of Migrant Labor: The Construction of National Identities in the USA and Britain." *Ethnic and Racial Studies* 19(1): 135-157.

Chiswick, Barry R. 1992. "Immigrants in the U.S. Local Labor Market." *Annals of the American Academy of Political and Social Sciences* 460 (March): 64-72.

Claiborne, Louis, Julian Friedman, Bradford Cooke, Kuttan Menon and David Stephen. 1983. *Race and Law in Britain and the United States.* 3rd edition. London: Minority Rights Group.

Cross, Malcolm. 1992. "Introduction: Migration, the City and the Urban Dispossessed." Page 1 to 16 in *Ethnic Minorities and Industrial Change in Europe and North America.* Edited by Malcolm Cross. Cambridge: Cambridge University Press.

Daneshvary, Nasser and R. Keith Schwer. 1994. "Black Immigrants in the U.S. Labor Market: An Earnings Analysis." *Review of Black Political Economy* 22(Winter): 77-98.

Danziger, Sheldon and Peter Gottschalk. 1995. *America Unequal.* New York/Cambridge: Russell Sage/Harvard.

Dodoo, F. Nii-Amoo. 1991a. "Immigrant and Native Black Workers' Labor Force Participation in the U.S." *National Journal of Sociology* 5(1): 3-17.

Dodoo, F. Nii-Amoo. 1991b. "Earnings Differentials among Blacks in America." *Social Science Research* 20(2): 93-108.

Dodoo, F. Hii-Amoo. 1997. "Assimilation Differences among Africans in America." *Social Forces* 76(2): 527-546.

Dorling, Daniel. 1995. *A New Social Atlas of Britain.* New York: John Wiley and Sons.

Driedger, Leo. 1989. "Alternate Models of Assimilation, Integration and Pluralism." Pg. 349-360 in *Canada 2000: Race Relations and Public Policy.* Edited by O.P. Dwivedi, Ronald D'Costa, C. Lloyd Stanford, and Elliott Tepper. Guelph, Canada: Univ. of Guelph.

Duncan, Otis D. 1961. "A Socioeconomic Index for All Occupations" and "Properties and Characteristics of the Socioeconomic Index." Pg. 109-161 in *Occupations and Social Status.* Edited by A.J. Reiss, Jr. Glencoe, IL: Free Press.

Edmonston, Barry. 1996. *Statistics on U.S. Immigration.* National Research Council. Washington, D.C.: National Academy Press.

Elliott, Jean Leonard and Augie Fleras. 1990. "Immigration and the Canadian Ethnic Mosaic." Pg. 51-76 in *Race and Ethnic Relations in Canada*. Edited by Peter S. Li. Toronto: Oxford University Press.

Espenshade, Thomas J. and Charles A. Calhoun. 1993. "An Analysis of Public Opinion Toward Undocumented Immigration." *Population Research and Policy Review* 12: 189-224.

Esping-Andersen, Gosta. 1990. *The Three Worlds of Welfare Capitalism*. Cambridge: Polity Press.

Esping-Andersen, Gøsta (editor). 1993. *Changing Classes: Stratification and Mobility in Post-Industrial Societies*. Sage Studies in International Sociology #45. Newbury Park, CA and London: Sage.

Farley, Reynolds and Walter R. Allen. 1987. "Race, Ancestry, and Socioeconomic Status: Are West Indian Blacks More Successful?" Ch. 12 in *The Color Line and the Quality of Life in America*. New York: Russell Sage Foundation.

Fawcett, James T. and Fred Arnold. 1987. "Explaining Diversity: Asian and Pacific Immigration Systems." Pg. 453-473 in *Pacific Bridges*. Edited by J.T. Fawcett and B.V. Carino. NY: Center for Migration Studies.

Foner, Nancy. 1983. "Jamaican Immigrants: A Comparative Analysis of the New York and London Experience." Occasional Paper no. 36. New York University: New York Research Program in Inter-American Affairs.

Foner, Nancy. 1986. "Sex Roles and Sensibilities: Jamaican Women in New York and London." Ch. 8 in *International Migration: The Female Experience*. Edited by Rita James Simon and Caroline B. Brettell. New Jersey: Rowman and Allanheld.

Freeman, Gary P. 1987. "Caribbean Migration to Britain and France: From Assimilation to Selection." Pg. 185-203 in *The Caribbean Exodus*. Edited by Barry B. Levine. New York: Praeger.

Frey, William and Aldin Speare. 1992. "The Revival of Metropolitan Population Growth in the U.S." *Population and Development Review* 18: 129-146.

Gans, Herbert J. 1992. "Second-Generation Decline: Scenarios of the the Economic and Ethnic Futures of the Post-1965 American Immigrants." *Ethnic and Racial Studies* 15(2): 172-192.

Ganzeboom, Harry, Paul DeGraaf and Donald Treiman. 1992. "A Standard Socio-Economic Index of Occupational Status." *Social Science Research* 21: 1-56.

Ganzeboom, Harry and Donald Treiman. 1996. "Internationally Comparable Measures of Occupational Status for the 1988 International Standard Classification of Occupations." *Social Science Research* 25: 201-239.

Gershuny, Jonathan. 1993. "Post-industrial Career Structures in Britain." Chapter 6 in *Changing Classes: Stratification and Mobility in Post-Industrial*

Societies. Edited by Gosta Esping-Andersen. Sage Studies in International Sociology #45. Newbury Park, CA and London: Sage.

Gilbertson, Greta. 1995. "Women's Labor and Enclave Employment: The Case of Dominican and Colombian Women in New York City." *International Migration Review* 29(3): 657-670.

Gober, Patricia. 1993. *Americans on the Move.* Population Bulletin vol. 48, no. 3.

Gordon, Milton. 1964. *Assimilation in American Life.* New York: Oxford University Press.

Gordon, Monica H. 1990. "Dependents or Independent Workers? : The Status of Caribbean Immigrant Women in the United States." Ch. 6 from *In Search of a Better Life: Perspectives on Migration from the Caribbean.* Edited by Ransford W. Palmer. New York: Praeger.

Green, Anne. 1997. Chapter 4 in *Ethnicity in the 1991 Census, vol 4: Employment, Education and Housing among the Ethnic Minority Populations of Britain.* Edited by Valerie Karn. London: The Stationery Office.

Hacker, Andrew. 1992. *Two Nations: Black and White, Separate, Hostile, Unequal.* New York: Charles Scribner's Sons (Macmillan Publishing Company).

Hamnett, Chris and Bill Randolph. 1992. "Racial Minorities in the London Labour and Housing Markets: A Longitudinal Analysis, 1971-1981." Chapter 8 in *Ethnic Minorities and Industrial Change in Europe and North America.* Edited by Malcolm Cross. Cambridge: Cambridge University Press.

Harwood, Edwin. 1986. "American Public Opinion and U.s. Immigration Policy: Changing Attitudes Toward Both Legal and Illegal Immigration." *Annals of the American Academy of Political and Social Science* 487: 201-12 S

Hauser, Robert M. and John Robert Warren. 1997. "Socioeconomic Indexes for Occupations: A Review, Update, and Critique." *Sociological Methodology* 27: 177-251.

Heckman, James J. 1979. "Sample Selection Bias as a Specification Error." *Econometrica* 47(1): 153-160.

Hennessy, Alistair. 1988. "Workers of the Night: West Indians in Britain." Ch. 2 in *Lost Illusions: Caribbean Migrants in Britain and the Netherlands.* Edited by Malcolm Cross and Hans Entzinger. London: Routledge.

Henry, Frances. 1987. "Caribbean Migration to Canada: Prejudice and Opportunity." Pg. 214-222 in *The Caribbean Exodus.* Edited by Barry B. Levine. New York: Praeger.

Henry, Frances. 1994. *The Caribbean Diaspora in Toronto: Learning to Live with Racism.* Toronto: University of Toronto Press.

Jacobs, Jerry. 1993. "Careers in the US Service Economy." Chapter 8 in *Changing Classes: Stratification and Mobility in Post-Industrial Societies.* Edited by Gosta Esping-Andersen. Sage Studies in International Sociology #45. Newbury Park, CA and London: Sage.

Jackman, Mary. 1994. *The Velvet Glove: Paternalism and Conflict in Gender, Class and Race Relations.* Berkeley: University of California Press.

James, Rita and Susan H. Alexander. 1993. *The Ambivalent Welcome, Print Media, Public Opinion, and Immigration.* Westport, Conn.,: Praeger.

Kalmijn, Matthijs. 1996. "The Socioeconomic Assimilation of Caribbean American Blacks." *Social Forces* 74(3): 911-930.

Karn, Valerie (editor). 1997. *Ethnicity in the 1991 Census, vol 4: Employment, Education and Housing among the Ethnic Minority Populations of Britain.* London: The Stationery Office.

Kasinitz, Philip. 1992. *Caribbean New York: Black Immigrants and the Politics of Race.* Ithaca, New York: Cornell University.

King, Mary. 1995. "Black Women's Labor Market Status: Occupational Segregation in the United States and Great Britain." *Review of Black Political Economy* 24(1): 23-43.

Ko, Gilbert Kwok-Yiu and Clifford C. Clogg. 1986. "Earnings Differential between Chinese and Whites in 1980: Subgroup Variability and Evidence for Convergence." *Social Science Research* 18: 249-270.

Li, Peter S. 1988. *Ethnic Inequality in a Class Society.* Toronto: Wall and Thompson.

Li, Peter S. 1990. "Race and Ethnicity." Pg. 1-15 in *Race and Ethnic Relations in Canada.* Edited by Peter S. Li. Toronto: Oxford University Press.

Marshall, Dawn. 1987. "A History of West Indian Migrations: Overseas Opportunities and 'Safety Valve' Policies." Pg. 15-31 in *The Caribbean Exodus.* Edited by Barry B. Levine. New York: Praeger.

Mason, David J. 1995. *Race and Ethnicity in Modern Britain.* Oxford: Oxford University Press.

Massey, Douglas, Joaquin Arango, Graeme Hugo, Ali Kouaouci, Adela Pellegrino, and J. Edward Taylor. 1993. "Theories of International Migration: A Review and Appraisal." *Population and Development Review* 19(3): 431-466.

Model, Suzanne. 1991. "Caribbean Immigrants: A Black Success Story?" *International Migration Review* 25(2): 248-276.

Model, Suzanne and David Ladipo. 1996. "Context and Opportunity: Minorities in London and New York." *Social Forces* 75(2): 485-510.

Model, Suzanne. 1997. "Black Immigrants in Three White Societies." Paper presented at the Annual Meeting of the American Sociological Association. Toronto, Canada.

Myles, John, Garnett Picot and Ted Wannell. 1993. "Does Post-Industrialism Matter? The Canadian Experience." Chapter 7 in *Changing Classes: Stratification and Mobility in Post-Industrial Societies.* Edited by Gosta Esping-Andersen. Sage Studies in International Sociology #45. Newbury Park, CA and London: Sage.

Muller, Luttinger, Konig and Karle. 1990. "Class and Education in Industrial Nations." Ch. 3 in *Class Structure in Europe.* Edited by Max Haller. New York: Armonk.

Nakao, Keiko and Judith Treas. 1994. "Updating Occupational Prestige and Socioeconomic Scores: How the New Measures Measure Up." *Sociological Methodology* 24: 1-72.

Nee, Victor, Jimy M. Sanders, and Scott Sernau. 1994. "Job Transitions in an Immigrant Metropolis: Ethnic Boundaries and the Mixed Economy." *American Sociological Review* 59(December): 849-872.

Noble, Trevor. 1981. *Structure and Change in Modern Britain.* London: Bastford Academic and Educational Ltd.

Office of Population Censuses and Surveys/General Register Office for Scotland (OPCS). 1991a. 1991 Census Local Base Statistics/Small Area Statistics, Data tables. Hampshire, Great Britain: Office for National Statistics.

Office of Population Censuses and Surveys/General Register Office for Scotland (OPCS). 1991b. *1991 Census User Guide* Nos. 9, 24, 38, and 48. Hampshire, Great Britain: Office for National Statistics.

Office of Population Censuses and Surveys/General Register Office for Scotland (OPCS). 1992. *1991 Census: Definitions, Great Britain.* London: Her Majesty's Stationery Office.

Oliver, Melvin L. and Thomas M. Shapiro. 1995. *Black Wealth/White Wealth: A New Perspective on Racial Inequality.* New York and London: Routledge.

Olzak, Susan. 1992. *Dynamics of Ethnic Competition and Conflict.* Stanford University Press.

Openshaw, Stan. (editor). 1995. *Census Users' Handbook.* New York: John Wiley & Sons.

Owen, David. 1997. "Labour Force Participation Rates, Self-Employment and Unemployment." Chapter 3 in *Ethnicity in the 1991 Census, vol 4: Employment, Education and Housing among the Ethnic Minority Populations of Britain.* Edited by Valerie Karn. London: The Stationery Office.

Palmer, Ransford W. 1995. *Pilgrims from the Sun: West Indian Migration to America.* New York: Twayne.

Pedraza, Silvia. 1991. "Women and Migration: The Social Consequences of Gender." *Annual Review of Sociology* 17: 303-325.

Portes, Alejando. 1987. "One Field, Many Views: Competing Theories on International Migration." Pg. 53-70 in *Pacific Bridges*. Edited by J.T. Fawcett and B.V. Carino. NY: Center for Migration Studies.

Portes, Alejandro and Jozsef Borocz. 1989. "Contemporary Immigration: Theoretical Perspectives on its Determinants and Modes of Incorporation." *International Migration Review* 23(3): 606-630.

Portes, Alejandro and Min Zhou. 1992. "Gaining the Upper Hand: Economic Mobility Among Immigrant and Domestic Minorities." *Ethnic and Racial Studies* 15(4): 491-522.

Portes, Alejandro and Min Zhou. 1993. "The New Second Generation: Segmented Assimilation and Its Variants." *Annals of the American Academy of Political and Social Sciences* 530 (November): 74-96.

Portes, Alejandro and Ramon Grosfoguel. 1994. "Caribbean Diasporas: Migration and Ethnic Communities." *Annals of the American Academy of Political and Social Sciences* 533 (May): 48-69.

Portes, Alejandro (editor). 1995. *Economic Sociology and the Sociology of Immigration*. New York: Russell Sage.

Poston, Jr., Dudley L. 1994. "Patterns of Economic Attainment of Foreign-Born Male Workers in the United States." *International Migration Review* 28(3): 478-499.

Reid, Junior. 1986. "Foreign Mind." Jamaican popular song.

Reitz, Jeffrey G. 1988. "The Institutional Structure of Immigration as a Determinant of Inter-Racial Competition: A Comparison of Britain and Canada." *International Migration Review* 22(1): 117-146.

Reitz, Jeffrey G. 1998. *Warmth of the Welcome: The Social Causes of Economic Success for Immigrants in Different Nations and Cities*. Colorado: Westview Press.

Reskin, Barbara. 1990. *Job Queues, Gender Queues*. Temple University Press.

Richmond, Anthony H. 1990. "Race Relations and Immigration: A Comparative Perspective." *International Journal of Comparative Sociology* 31(3-4): 156-176.

Richmond, Anthony H. 1992. "Immigration and Structural Change: The Canadian Experience, 1971-1986." *International Migration Review* 26: 1200-1221.

Rindfuss, Ronald R., Karin L. Brewster, and Andrew L. Kavee. 1996. "Women, Work, and Children: Behavioral and Attitudinal Change in the United States." *Population and Development Review* 22(3): 457-482.

Robinson, Vaughan. 1990. "Roots to Mobility: The Social Mobility of Britain's Black Population, 1971-1987." *Ethnic and Racial Studies* 13(2): 274-286.

Samuel, T.J. and B. Woloski. 1985. "The Labour Market Experiences of Canadian Immigrants." *International Migration* 23(2): 225-250.

Sample of Anonymised Records (SARS) from the 1991 Census of Population of Great Britain. Data: 1% Household File and 2% Individual File. Census Microdata Unit, the University of Manchester with the support of ESRC/JISC/DENI.

Sample of Anonymised Records (SARS) from the 1991 Census of Population of Great Britain. 1996. *Codebook for the 1% Household File and 2% Individual File.* Census Microdata Unit, the University of Manchester with the support of ESRC/JISC/DENI.

Sassen, Saskia. 1995. "Immigration and Local Labor Markets." Ch. 3 in *The Economic Sociology of Immigration.* Edited by Alejandro Portes. New York: Russell Sage Foundation.

Segal, Aaron. 1987. "The Caribbean Exodus in a Global Context: Comparative Migration Experiences." Pg. 44-64 in *The Caribbean Exodus.* Edited by Barry B. Levine. New York: Praeger.

Semyonov, M., D.R. Hoyt and R.I. Scott. 1984. "Place, Race and Differential Occupational Opportunities." *Demography* 21: 259-270.

Simmons, Alan B. and Kiernan Keohane. 1992. "Canadian Immigration Policy: State Strategies and the Quest for Legitimacy." *Canadian Review of Sociology and Anthropology* 29(4): 265-452.

Solomos, John. 1989. *Race and Racism in Contemporary Britain.* London: Macmillian.

Stafford, James. 1992. "Welcome but Why? Recent Changes in Canadian Immigration Policy." *American Review of Canadian Studies* 22(2): 235-258.

Stanfield, John H, II. 1991. "Racism in America and in Other Race-Centered Nation-States: Synchronic Considerations." *International Journal of Comparative Sociology* 32(3-4): 243-260.

Stasiulis, Davia. 1990. "Theorizing Connections: Gender, Race, Ethnicity." Pg. 269-305 in *Race and Ethnic Relations in Canada.* Edited by Peter S. Li. Toronto: Oxford University Press.

Statistics Canada. 1992a. *1991 Census Dictionary.* 1991 Census of Canada. Ottawa, Canada: Supply and Services Canada.

Statistics Canada. 1992b. 1991 Census Public Use Microdata File: Individual File (CD-ROM). 1991 Census of Canada. Ottawa, Canada.

Statistics Canada. 1992c. *Basic Summary Tabulations 100% Data.* Data and Documentation. Ottawa, Canada.

Statistics Canada. 1993. *Basic Summary Tabulations, 1991 - 20% Data.* Data and Documentation. Ottawa, Canada.

Statistics Canada. 1994. *User Documentation for Public Use Microdata File on Individuals.* 1991 Census of Canada. Ottowa: Statistics Canada.

Stevens, Gillian and David L. Featherman. 1981. "A Revised Socioeconomic Index of Occupational Status." *Social Science Research* 10: 364-395.

Stolzenberg, Ross M. and Daniel A. Relles. 1997. "Tools for Intuition About Sample Selection Bias and its Correction." *American Sociological Review* 62 (June): 494-507.

Tickamyer, Ann R. 1992. "The Working Poor in Rural Labor Markets: The Example of the Southeastern United States." Ch. 3 in *Rural Poverty in America.* Edited by Cynthia M. Duncan. Westport, Conn.: Auburn House.

Tickamyer, Ann R. and Janet Bokemeier. 1993. "Alternative Strategies for Labor Market Analyses: Multi-level Models of Labor Market Inequality." Ch. 4 in *Inequalities in Labor Market Areas.* Edited by Joachim Singelmann and Forrest A. Deseran. Boulder: Westview Press.

Thomas-Hope, Elizabeth M. 1986. "Caribbean Diaspora, the Inheritance of Slavery: Migration from the Commonwealth Caribbean." Ch. 2 in *The Caribbean in Europe: Aspects of the West Indian Experience in Britain, France and the Netherlands.* Edited by Colin Brock. London: Frank Cass.

Tootle, Deborah M. and Leann M. Tigges. 1993. "Black Concentration and Underemployment in Southern Labor Markets." Ch. 12 in *Inequalities in Labor Market Areas.* Edited by Joachim Singelmann and Forrest A. Deseran. Boulder: Westview Press.

Troper, Harold. 1993. "Canada's Immigration Policy Since 1945." *International Journal* 48(2): 255-279.

Ujimoto, K. Victor. 1990. "Studies of Ethnic Identity and Race Relations." Pg. 209-230 in *Race and Ethnic Relations in Canada.* Edited by Peter S. Li. Toronto: Oxford University Press.

Verma, R.B.P. and K.G. Basavarajappa. 1989. "Employment Income of Immigrants in Metropolitan Areas of Canada, 1980." *International Migration* 27(3): 441-465.

Walker, James W. 1989. "'Race' Policy in Canada: A Prospective." Pg. 1-19 in *Canada 2000: Race Relations and Public Policy.* Edited by O.P. Dwivedi, Ronald D'Costa, C. Lloyd Stanford, and Elliott Tepper. Guelph, Canada: Univ. of Guelph.

Wilson, William Julius. 1996. *When Work Disappears: The World of the New Urban Poor.* New York: Alfred A. Knopf.

Index

Printed in the United States
2097